JOHN SCOTTUS ERIUGENA

GREAT MEDIEVAL THINKERS

Series Editor

Brian Davies
Blackfriars, University of Oxford,
and Fordham University

Duns Scotus
Richard Cross

Bernard of Clairvaux
Gillian R. Evans

Boethius
John A. Marenbon

John Scottus Eriugena
Deirdre Carabine

JOHN SCOTTUS ERIUGENA

Deirdre Carabine

NEW YORK   OXFORD

OXFORD UNIVERSITY PRESS

2000

Oxford University Press

Oxford　New York

Athens　Auckland　Bangkok　Bogotá　Buenos Aires　Calcutta
Cape Town　Chennai　Dar es Salaam　Delhi　Florence　Hong Kong　Istanbul
Karachi　Kuala Lumpur　Madrid　Melbourne　Mexico City　Mumbai
Nairobi　Paris　São Paulo　Singapore　Taipei　Tokyo　Toronto　Warsaw

And associated companies in
Berlin　Ibadan

Copyright © 2000 by Deirdre Carabine

Published by Oxford University Press, Inc.
198 Madison Avenue, New York, New York 10016

Oxford is a registered trademark of Oxford University Press, Inc.

Library of Congress Cataloging-in-Publication Data
Carabine, Deirdre.
John Scottus Eriugena / Deirdre Carabine.
p.　cm. — (Great medieval thinkers)
Includes bibliographical references and index.
ISBN 0-19-511361-6; ISBN 0-19-511362-4 (pbk.)
1. Erigena, Johannes Scotus, ca. 810-ca. 877.
2. Philosophy, Medieval.　I. Title.　II. Series.
B765.J34C27　2000
189—dc21　99-29192

1 3 5 7 9 8 6 4 2

Printed in the United States of America
on acid-free paper

IN MEMORIAM
JOHN PRESS CARABINE
1928–1999

PREFACE

This book is intended to serve as an introduction to the ideas of the ninth-century Irish philosopher John Scottus Eriugena. It requires no special knowledge of Eriugena nor of medieval philosophy, but it will, I hope, also be of interest to more experienced readers. A short introduction to Eriugena's thought cannot possibly offer a comprehensive account of the many ideas and concepts he himself grappled with during his short but fairly prolific literary career. Unfortunately, I have found it necessary to omit discussion of many themes that could have found a place this volume. I have not, for example, dealt specifically with Eriugena's more theological works, and I have examined neither the various commentaries he wrote nor some of the more peripheral themes of the *Periphyseon*. Eriugena was a polymath and an exceptional philosopher, notwithstanding the fact that he lived in what has, until fairly recently, been described as the "dark ages." In this book I have chosen themes and concepts that will, I believe, give the reader a fairly accurate picture of his philosophical and theological interests.

I wish to acknowledge the debt I owe to my mentor and father in Neoplatonism, Arthur Hilary Armstrong. Many others have had a hand in shaping the ideas that have found their way into this book: James McEvoy, Werner Beierwaltes, and Dermot Moran (who first introduced me to the exciting ideas of Eriugena). The careful scrutiny of Philipp Rosemann and Tom O'Loughlin has eliminated many errors from the text, and I am grateful for their critical comments, suggestions, and friendship.

The tropical heat of the equator, tempered by the cooling breezes of Lake Victoria, full of the bright light of a strong sun, seems a strange location for the author of a book on a ninth-century philosopher who lived in a very different, much colder world. The one commonality we share is that both of us are part of the Irish diaspora in lands where "there is no wine for the hot dry throats of the Irish."[1]

SERIES FOREWORD

Many people would be surprised to be told that there *were* any great medieval thinkers. If a *great* thinker is one from whom we can learn today, and if "medieval" serves as an adjective for describing anything that existed from (roughly) the years 600 to 1500 AD, then—so it is often supposed—medieval thinkers cannot be called "great."

But why not? One answer often given appeals to ways in which medieval authors with a taste for argument and speculation tend to invoke "authorities," especially religious ones. Such invocation of authority is not the stuff of which great thought is made—so it is often said today. It is also frequently said that greatness is not to be found in the thinking of those who lived before the rise of modern science, not to mention that of modern philosophy and theology. Students of science are nowadays hardly ever referred to literature earlier than the seventeenth century. Students of philosophy in the twentieth century have often been taught nothing about the history of ideas between Aristotle (384–22 BC) and Descartes (1596–1650). Modern students of theology have often been frequently encouraged to believe that significant theological thinking is a product of the nineteenth century.

Yet the origins of modern science lie in the conviction that the world is open to rational investigation and is orderly rather than chaotic—a conviction that came fully to birth, and was systematically explored and developed, during the Middle Ages. And it is in medieval thinking that we find some of the most sophisticated and rigorous discussions in the areas of philosophy and theology ever offered for human consumption. This is, perhaps, not surprising if we note that medieval philosophers and theologians, like their contemporary counterparts, were mostly university teachers, participating in an ongoing debate with contributors from different countries and—unlike many seventeenth-, eighteenth-, and even nineteenth-century philosophers and theologians—did not work in relative isolation from the community of teachers and students with whom they were regularly involved. As for the question of appeal to authority: It is certainly true that many medieval thinkers believed in authority (especially religious authority) as a serious court of appeal; and it is true that most people today would say that they cannot do this. Yet authority is as much an ingredient in our thinking as it was for medieval thinkers. For most of what we take ourselves to know derives from the trust we have reposed in our various teachers, colleagues, friends, and general contacts. When it comes to reliance on authority, the main difference between us and medieval thinkers lies in the fact that their reliance on authority (insofar as they had it) was often more focused and explicitly acknowledged than is ours. It does not lie in the fact that it was uncritical and naive in a way that our reliance on authority is not.

In recent years, such truths have come to be increasingly recognized at what we might call the "academic" level. No longer disposed to think of the Middle Ages as "dark" (meaning "lacking in intellectual richness"), many university departments (and many publishers of books and journals) now devote a lot of their energy to the study of medieval thinking. And they do so not simply on the assumption that it is historically significant. They do so in the light of the increasingly developing insight that it is full of things with which to dialogue and from which to learn. Following a long period in which medieval thinking was thought to be of only antiquarian interest, we are now witnessing its revival as a contemporary voice—one to converse with, one from which we might learn.

The *Great Medieval Thinkers* series reflects and is part of this exciting revival. Written by a distinguished team of experts, it aims to provide substantial introductions to a range of medieval authors. And it does so on the assumption that they are as worth reading today as they were when they wrote. Students of medieval "literature" (e.g., the writings of Chaucer) are currently well supplied (if not over supplied) with secondary works to aid them when reading the objects of their concern. But those with an interest in medieval philosophy and theology are by no means so fortunate when it comes to reliable and accessible volumes to help them. The *Great Medieval Thinkers* series therefore aspires to remedy that deficiency by concentrating on medieval philosophers and theologians, coupled with modern reflection on what they had to say. Taken individually, volumes in the series will provide valuable treatments of single thinkers, many of whom are not currently covered by any comparable volumes. Taken together, they will constitute a rich and distinguished history and discussion of medieval philosophy and theology considered as a whole. With an eye on college and university students, and with an eye on the general reader, authors of volumes in the series write in a clear and accessible manner so that each of the thinkers they write on can be learned about by those who have no previous knowledge of them. Each contributor to the series will also strive to inform, engage, and generally entertain even those with specialist knowledge in the area of medieval thinking. So, as well as surveying and introducing, volumes in the series will advance the state of medieval studies both at the historical and the speculative level.

Little is known about the life of the subject of the present volume, the ninth-century Irishman John Scottus Eriugena. But his significance as a thinker is now commonly acknowledged by all serious medievalists. Translator, exegete, theologian, and philosopher, Eriugena is one of the greatest of Christian Neoplatonists. Along with figures like Maimonides (1135–1204) and Aquinas (c.1225–74), he is also one of the most distinguished practitioners of negative theology—the attempt to safeguard the transcendence of God by stressing the limits of human understanding, by reminding us of what God cannot be. In this respect he resembles some of the authors who clearly had an impact on him, writers like St. Augustine of Hippo (354–430), Dionysius the Areopagite (c.500), Gregory of Nyssa (c.330–c.395), and Maximus the Confessor (c.580–662).

Eriugena's thinking united Greek East and Latin West at a time when learning had reached a low point. And he came under suspicion of heresy for many centuries. In this book, however, Deirdre Carrabine illustrates the extent to which his thinking is thoroughly Christian while also being innovative, daring, and surprisingly modern. In doing so, she concentrates on Eriugena's greatest work, the *Periphyseon* (also known by the title *De divisione naturae*). But she also ranges over Eriugena's other writings. She provides a first-class introduction to her subject, one which well fulfills the aims of the series to which it belongs. Those who know her book *The Unknown God* (Louvain, 1995) will realize that she is an expert on negative theology from Plato to Eriugena. In the present volume she displays all of the learning to be found in her earlier work while focussing on the thinker with which it ends. I warmly commend it to readers as a fine study of a subtle and original mind.

Brian Davies
Series Editor

CONTENTS

PART I · INTRODUCTION

THE WORLD OF THE
NINTH CENTURY

When Charles Martel defeated the Arabs at Tours in 732, he laid the central foundation stone for the establishment of the great Carolingian dynasty that was to become the focal point of the ninth-century revival of learning. His son, Pepin III, ascended the throne in 741, but it was his grandson, Charles the Great, Charlemagne (742–814), king of the Franks at the early age of twenty-one and subsequently reigning for the next forty-six years, who put the Frankish kingdom on the intellectual map. In A.D. 800, when Charlemagne was crowned head of the Holy Roman Empire by Pope Leo III in Rome, a new era had reached its noontime for the intellectual life of western Europe. The long reign of Charlemagne, a Christian monarch in a new mold and legitimized by divine grace, represents a bright period in the history of Western philosophy and culture. Charlemagne was the first of a trinity of "priestly kings" to whom the intellectual life of the West is hugely indebted; his son Louis and his grandson Charles complete the trio.

The intellectual awakening of the ninth century, which was instigated by Charlemagne, is known as the Carolingian revival or renaissance. This *renovatio* is best remembered as a blossoming of the arts and intellectual life, but it can also be categorized as an era in which the whole of society was remodeled: Charlemagne attempted to organize his kingdom in the manner in which he had organized his court. According to historian David Knowles: "Seen from a distance in the perspective of history, the Carolingian revival is . . . a patch of sunlight rather brighter than the others [revivals] which in its turn disappeared in a swirl of mist."[1] However, this intellectual and cultural revival must be seen in the context of the everyday world of social, political, economic, military, and theological controversy. Ninth-century Europe was fraught with new and with lingering controversies, disputes, and wars. There is a tendency to see the Carolingian period of the eighth and ninth centuries as a period of sunshine in the intellectual night that had persisted since the fall of the Roman Empire and the demise of classical learning, but against the background of a blossoming intellectualism, Charlemagne himself spent his long reign fighting aggressive wars and settling troublesome political disputes. He annexed the Lombard Kingdom, the Duchy of Bavaria, the Duchy of Spoleto, and a strip of northern Spain as a buffer against the Arabs to the south. He had subdued the Saxons and Frisians—his aims did not include Celtic and Anglo-Saxon lands—and there was an increasing threat from Viking raids on his shores. He was a brilliant military strategist, and under his rule the Frankish kingdom can be said to have truly become an empire.

The court of Charlemagne was largely itinerant, visiting, in turn, Aachen (Aix-la-Chapelle), Reims, Laon, and Compiègne (where Charles the Bald established himself as emperor in 876), but at Aachen Charlemagne finally settled toward the end of his life, and he was buried there in 814. The palace at Aachen and Odo of Metz's octagonal church constructed by Charlemagne and consecrated by Pope Leo III in 805, in imitation of Rome and Byzantium, can be said to symbolize, at least in part, this revival of learning, which had at its core Christian learning. Charlemagne, like his grandson Charles the Bald, was enamored with things Byzantine,[2] a liking that possibly assisted the dissemination of the works of the Eastern writer the Pseudo-Dionysius, which Eriugena translated at Charles's request. In fact, Charles himself built a church that was a replica of the Aachen church (Notre Dame at Compiègne); some scholars believe Eriugena's long poem *Aulae sidereae* may refer to this church.[3]

When his son Louis died in 840, the great empire of Charlemagne that had begun so spectacularly began its slow collapse. In 843, the empire divided between the three grandsons of Charlemagne into Aquitaine, Italy, and Bavaria, corresponding, very roughly, to what we now know as France, Italy, and Germany. However, while the great political edifice began its collapse in 843, the educational reforms and the general revival of learning survived, though not without some brief depressions.

The Intellectual Revival

Charlemagne's efforts to create a culture for the Christian Empire he had built centered upon the scriptures and classical humanism and is generally signaled by the famous capitulary of 789 (the *Admonitio generalis*), in which the king advised that all cathedrals and monasteries were to open schools dedicated to the study of the psalms, musical notation, chant, computistics, and grammar. This does not suggest, however, that such schools did not exist: episcopal and monastic schools were already centres of learning, especially at St. Gall, Corbie, Reichenau, and Fulda (where Hrabanus Maurus became abbot in 822). Also indicated in Charlemagne's capitulary was a strong recommendation to acquire faithful and accurate copies of the texts of the scriptures. Thus, the production of books became an extremely important activity of the time; the proliferation of richly decorated illuminated texts, especially from Corbie, bears witness to this fact (one of the finest examples is the Lothar Gospels prepared by the monastery of Tours). Copying and reading texts became a much easier task with the evolution of what we now refer to as Carolingian minuscule. Therefore, while secular learning was extremely important in the Carolingian renovatio, the scriptures acted as the preeminent guide in the remodeling of Frankish learning and society. Charlemagne also ordered the revision of the Vulgate associated with the name of Alcuin of York, who was instrumental in facilitating his sovereign's call for the implementation of a system of learning upon his arrival at the royal court in 782.

Alcuin's vision of the progress of learning was based upon the fathers of the church, the study of the scriptures, and the remodeling of classical learning and education. It was largely Alcuin's vision of creating "in France a new Athens," that consolidated the role of the Frankish king Charles as Charlemagne, Holy Roman Emperor who had the power to protect and nurture the Church. According to the model of Alcuin, the emperor Charlemagne (often compared with Constantine) had both a political and a theological mandate; it could be said that his duty to protect the Church was greater even than the duty and power of the pope. Indeed, this trinity of rulers in Carolingian times exercised their religious duties seriously and, in their interactions with popes and bishops, involved themselves in theology and religious disputes as much as in other aspects of courtly life. Charlemagne's theological or religious mandate can be seen in the fact that he was often referred to as David in his court, although he liked to think of himself as Josiah. "In restoring the law of the book to his society, Charlemagne wished to become a Frankish king like no other, a king like Josiah."[4] Alcuin actively promoted such a conception of his king.

It was Alcuin who laid the foundations for the ninth-century understanding of the liberal arts (relying heavily on Martianus Capella and Boethius) and with others (Theodulf of Orleans, Paul of Lombard, and Hrabanus Maurus) promoted their study.[5] The accepted classification of the liberal arts was prompted by the allegory *Marriage of Mercury and Philology* by Martianus Capella, who probably lived in Roman North Africa in the early fifth century. According to the accepted classification, the *trivium* consisted of grammar, rhetoric, and dialectic, and the *quadrivium* consisted of arithmetic, geometry, astronomy, and music. At Alcuin's instigation, copies of the *Consolation of Philosophy* of Boethius were circulated, and the Carolingian study of the works of Boethius (himself a bridge between the Greek and Latin worlds) and Martianus Capella formed the core of the arts curriculum for some time to come. The adoption of Boethius's text was not without consequence, for it not only guided the educational curriculum but very firmly placed *philosophia*, the guide of reason, on the intellectual agenda, though not in any institutionalized fashion. While philosophy was not integrated into the Christian educational curriculum until the time of the founding of the universities, the emphasis on reason in Christian education signaled the beginning of a tradition that was to come to its full blossoming in the works of the thirteenth-century master Thomas Aquinas. Philosophy and Christianity could now come to a much more fruitful union, and the Christian could now follow legitimately Augustine's example and adopt philosophia as an official guide on the path to Christian wisdom. Thus, the arts became an indispensable part of Christian formation, and the spoils of the classicists were used by Carolingian scholars to the greatest effect. As in Augustine's conception, the seven liberal arts were regarded as gifts from God, the secular equivalent of the seven gifts of the spirit, which could assist the advance toward God more fruitfully than the reading of the scriptures alone. Although the works of Martianus and Boethius were the chief inspirations for ninth-century scholars, other authors also exerted an important influence on intellectual pursuits: Cassiodorus, Isidore of Seville, Macrobius, Cicero, Priscian, Porphyry, Lucan, Pliny, and some of Aristotle's logical texts.

The cosmopolitan group of scholars gathered to the courts of the Carolingian kings (Irish, Anglo-Saxons, and Italians), implemented Charlemagne's wishes on a scale that could hardly have been imagined. The nature of eighth- and ninth-century education—the study of the scriptures, the Latin authorities, classical authors, and the Greek fathers—had an effect on the whole culture of the Frankish kingdom. Charlemagne's lead was continued by his son and grandson, though with varying degrees of success. Louis the Pious had a more theological than military bent (Charles appears to have been more like his grandfather than his father), and when Louis was crowned emperor he convened councils at Aachen with church reforms and the settling of theological disputes in mind. In turn, Charles the Bald (823–877) was crowned emperor by Pope John VIII in St. Peter's at Rome on 25th December 875 (only two years before his death) on the anniversary of Charlemagne's coronation. At the right hand of each of these kings stood scholars. Just as his father had relied on Alcuin, Louis was advised by the reformer monk Benedict of Aniane and by Fredegisus, Alcuin's student. In turn, his son, Charles, who was tutored by Walafrid Strabo, also gathered scholars around him: Hincmar, the powerful bishop of Reims, and John Scottus Eriugena.

The Irish Connection

It is said that the second diaspora of Irish scholars from their homeland (the first were evangelizers) was caused by increasing incidences of Viking raids in Ireland. We can be sure then that Eriugena was not the only Irish scholar to have sought refuge in a safer land. However, the attraction of the king's court and the intellectual nature of courtly affairs must also have induced many scholars to leave their homelands, independent of hostility in their own countries. Despite the pioneering efforts of German scholars to prove that Ireland in the ninth century was still capable of producing high-quality scholars (a debate that continues today), earlier in this century Maïeul Cappuyns's view was that it was in the seventh century that Ireland truly deserved the title "land of saints and scholars."[6] It is true that the ninth century was a time of great misfortunes in Ireland as Scandinavians continued to wreak havoc on coastal regions. This devastation also took its toll on scholastic endeavors, and the great monastic centers of Bangor and Armagh were raided and left in ruins. Nevertheless, although Irish learning reached its heyday in the seventh and eighth centuries, scholarship was still an important aspect of life in the monastic centers of the ninth and later centuries. In Europe, the foundations of the Irish missionaries in Gaul and north Italy had already become cultural centers that carried on the tradition of learning and stressed the importance of the spiritual as well as the intellectual life.

Although the Irish influence in Carolingian times is difficult to pinpoint with complete accuracy, it is likely that Bede was influenced by the Irish at Jarrow and York, and this influence may have been passed on to Alcuin himself, who took an interest in the state of scholarly affairs in Ireland, as a letter to confrères there warning that standards of learning were in decline demonstrates.[7] Thanks to the scholarship of John Contreni and others, the Irish presence at kingly courts is now something more than a shadowy hypothesis.[8] The "Irish colony," especially at Laon, played a significant role in the establishment of a new intellectualism. Martin Hibernensis (819–75) played a crucial role at Laon, and Irish scribes and scholars most likely worked at a scriptorium there. Even though the question of where these Irish scholars received their education is still open for scholarly scrutiny, it is a fact that the Irish abroad were generally renowned for their learning, and Hiberno-Latin exegesis is one feature of the biblical scholarship of the Carolingian period.[9] The great quest to unravel the mysterious threads of Irish influence and connections in the Frankish kingdom is not at an end: scholarly detective work continues but is hampered by the shadows cast by intervening centuries. The numerous manuscripts from Laon in the tenth and eleventh centuries are indications that scholarship was still flourishing there, and in the twelfth century Anselm firmly established that the efforts of the Irish and others in the ninth century had not been in vain.

Theological Controversy

The ninth century can be characterized in many ways according to one's perspective and interest. From the point of view of the theologian, it was a time when old disputes flared up as theological speculation met with secular learning. The most important disputes that came to the fore in the later part of the eighth century were a mixture of old and new and concerned predestination, the Eucharist, the iconoclast controversy, the problem concerning the vision of God and the nature of hell, the debate on adoptionism, and the *filioque* problem. In fact, although the royal courts were generally well disposed to Byzantine ways and traditions, the *Libri carolini*, composed by Theodulf of Orléans at the behest of Charlemagne when Leo III sent the Nicene decision to the Frankish king (outlining the doctrinal implications of the final victory of the iconophiles in 843), display discernible anti-Greek sentiments, indicative of the struggle for supremacy between the two great centers. The Eucharistic controversy, which concerned whether the body of Christ was present in the Eucharist in truth or in mystery (spiritually), was linked to Eriugena, who was believed to have written a treatise *On the Body and Blood of the Lord,* now understood to have been by Ratramnus of Corbie (this treatise was formally condemned at the Council of Vercelli in 1050).

However, despite the variety of theological debates and controversies, Eriugena seems to have become involved formally in only one dispute, that concerning predestination, although his views on the question of the vision of God and the filioque controversy can be found in the *Periphyseon*. It was when Hincmar of Reims asked Eriugena to clarify the issues involved in the predestination debate around 851–52, that the Irishman entered the pages of intellectual history for the first time. He was already at the king's court when his views were sought on this most fiery of issues, which had already been burning for over a decade. Hrabanus Maurus and Ratramnus, along with Hincmar himself, had also contributed to the debate, which was sparked off by the Saxon monk Gottschalk of Orbais (a pupil of Hrabanus). Indeed, Gottschalk and Ratramnus were to be involved in other thorny theological debates, most notably concerning the Trinity, the Eucharist, and the question of the nature of the final vision of God. Many scholars of the time sided with Gottschalk, including Ratramnus, Lupus of Ferrières, Prudentius of Troyes, and Florus of Lyon, while on the opposing team were Hrabanus Maurus and Hincmar. The bishop of Reims (possibly also with Pardulus of Laon and Charles himself) commissioned the views of Eriugena, in the hope of settling the dispute once and for all. They were to be disappointed.

The problem of predestination as it surfaced in the ninth century was not a new problem and is one for which Augustine of Hippo bears some responsibility.[10] Augustine's position had been that human beings cannot will what is good without the action of divine grace. Since they are dependent upon grace, it follows that human beings cannot save themselves; that means, some people are predestined to salvation. According to Augustine, however, the faults of the wicked and their resulting damnation are their own responsibility. Gottschalk believed that it followed from Augustine's account that if some are predestined to salvation and heavenly bliss, then those who are not saved through the action of divine grace are predestined to hell and eternal damnation. This rather crude formulation of the principle of "double predestination" gives a very simple picture of the position of Gottschalk, who claimed to be elaborating the views of Augustine. One argument of Gottschalk was based on the absoluteness and unchangeability of God: since God cannot change, either God's mind or God's judgment, the judgment of those who will be damned or saved must be predestined. This formulation of divine predestination troubled Hincmar, whose pastoral concern was directed toward stamping out a fatalistic attitude among Christians. Hincmar's own view, that there is only predestination to heaven for the elect is, in fact, closer to the original view of Augustine, who stressed both the grace of God and the free will of human beings.

Eriugena's view, as he sets it out in the rather hastily written treatise *On Predestination*, is that because God is simple and unchangeable, there can be nothing at all that can be predestined.[11] Eriugena explains God's predestination as God's knowledge of the primordial causes. God cannot predestine the human will, and people are blessed or punished because of their own free will. Since the free will of human beings can be misused, sins must be the fault of individuals. Sin and evil, and the fact that some souls are damned, cannot imply a change in God or a defect in God's power; if we accept the view of Gottschalk, God is responsible for sin and evil. Eriugena's way out of this difficult position is based on the Neoplatonic idea that God as good is simply existence and, therefore, the opposite of non-being. Evil and sin are negations that do not, in fact, exist and cannot be caused by God. Thus, God cannot predestine any soul to damnation; rather, human sinfulness creates its own hell. As I show in chapter 4, in the *Periphyseon* Eriugena argues that lack of knowledge in God is not a defect; in fact, nothing in God (wisdom, power, being, or the ability to predestine) can be understood, precisely because God's essence is simple and unchangeable. Therefore, Eriugena concludes, salvation is open to all, a theme I discuss in relation to his conception of the final return in *Periphyseon* V. In addition to the arguments based on the dialectical understanding of being and non-being and the unity of God's nature, Eriugena also invokes the principles of negative theology in his answer to Gottschalk's heresy. Foreknowledge and predestination imply temporal notions in God, who transcends time. Since God is simple and unchanging, ideas, signs, and language cannot properly signify the divine nature (*On Predestination* IX, 390B).[12]

This was, in brief, the case Eriugena presented to Hincmar for scrutiny. However, since Eriugena had denied the possibility of the predestination of the elect to eternal bliss, he had committed the sin of contradicting the great Augustine; for this reason Hincmar ultimately rejected the treatise. But a more serious issue was the invocation of the philosophical (and secular) principles of dialectic; in fact, Prudentius later rebuked Eriugena for using non-Christian

sources and arguments in his refutation of Gottschalk's heresy. The dialectical approach to a theological question (an approach Eriugena was to use to
great effect in the *Periphyseon*), resulted in the rejection of the work by Hincmar, Prudentius, and Florus as "sophistry," and the treatise was eventually
condemned at the council of Valence in 855 and at Langres in 859. Despite
the disappointment of Eriugena's apparent failure, Hincmar did not let the
matter drop; in fact, he could be said to have persecuted Gottschalk until he
died. The stubborn Saxon monk did not recant his heresy and died unrecon-
ciled with and reviled by his church. Surprisingly, Eriugena did not suffer the
same fate, and his future was much brighter, most likely because he was pro-
tected by Charles.

With regard to the predestination controversy, perhaps the one major
point that demands further discussion is the fact that both Gottschalk and Eriugena claimed to be clarifying the ideas of Augustine himself. It would appear
that, like the sacred texts, the writings of Augustine were open to manifold
interpretations, a view that brings into question the use of the authority of
Augustine. In the case of the predestination debate, Eriugena's practical application of the Augustinian dictum that true philosophy is true religion had
disastrous consequences. Theology (the study of the scriptures and the fathers)
was neither ready nor willing to admit the secular science of dialectic into its
privileged arena. Yet Eriugena's endeavors in relation to the question of predestination showed very clearly that the authority of Augustine could be questioned; as Jaroslav Pelikan observes, "the Augustinian synthesis" with which
the previous centuries had been comfortable was now called into question.[13]
In this sense, Eriugena's treatise *On Predestination* prefigures one recurring
characteristic one finds in the *Periphyseon:* the reconciliation of the many authorities who influenced one of the greatest philosophical minds of the ninth
century.

ERIUGENA'S LIFE AND
INTELLECTUAL ACHIEVEMENTS

An Enigma

John the Scot, Scottus, John Scottus Eriugena, a man of many names, is now
generally referred to by the names John Scottus Eriugena. Eriugena means
"born of Ireland," and in the preface to his translations of the works of the
Pseudo-Dionysius, he refers to himself simply as Eriugena. This man of many
names has also been described in many ways throughout history: Neoplatonist, poet, mystic, philosopher, theologian, idealist, heretic. Henry Bett, in
one of the earliest monographs on Eriugena in English, described him as the
most considerable philosopher in the Western world between Augustine and
Aquinas but also remarked that he was the loneliest figure in the history of
European thought.[1] Much early scholarship on Eriugena tended to view him
very much in isolation from his context and tradition.[2] Since the middle of
the twentieth century, there has been considerable revision of our concept
of Eriugena's place in the history of ideas, especially in the light of scholarship focused on those centuries called the dark ages. There is now a more
correct tendency to see him as part of a tradition of scholarship, learning, and
intellectualism.

Despite the fastidious efforts of Cappuyns to establish a biography of Eriugena in his comprehensive volume on him, the one word that most aptly describes the Irishman is "enigmatic," and it is well deserved. Almost everything
we can say about Eriugena can be questioned: we do not know precisely when
he was born, and he is no longer heard of after 870.[3] He appears again in history only in connection with various controversies and legends. Perhaps because he bore a common name, there has been much confusion regarding his
life; for example, some later historians situate him as a contemporary of Bede
and Alcuin, an error copied by others. Some seventeenth-century scholars

believed him to have studied at Athens or in the East, and he has also been connected with the foundation of the universities of Oxford and Paris.[4]

Eriugena was born in the first quarter of the ninth century, and he arrived at the court of Charles the Bald in the 840s, whether, as William of Malmesbury suggests, because of Viking raids in Ireland is not certain, but it is most likely. He seems to have first worked as a teacher of the liberal arts at the palace school and is said to have been interested also in music and medicine. There is no specific reference to him being a cleric, although when chastising him for his views on predestination, Prudentius notes that he has no distinguished rank within the church.[5] That could, of course, mean that he was a simple monk, although no other document of the time makes reference to this fact. Scholars have generally concluded that after his involvement in the predestination debate, he spent the next few years reading the fathers of the church, both Latin and Greek. Such was his prowess in Greek that Charles requested him to translate the precious works of the Pseudo-Dionysius, a task that had already been undertaken by the monk Hilduin at St. Denis. Although the reputation for learning of Irish scholars was well known in the eighth and ninth centuries, there has been some considerable discussion on the question of where Eriugena received his education, more specifically where he learned Greek. The view of Cappuyns, which he could not have learned Greek in Ireland, was challenged by Ludwig Bieler and others, who were more optimistic that such learning would still have been possible in Ireland at that time.[6] This discussion has not been concluded. The important fact is that Eriugena was able to read Greek, not only because of the translations he made but also because in his own work, the *Periphyseon*, we find a masterly knowledge of Eastern and Western authorities. Given the court predilection for things Greek, there is no doubt that because of Eriugena's linguistic abilities he would have found great favor with his king and patron; he was on extremely good terms with Charles, if the stories related by William of Malmesbury are true.

As to the reason why he is no longer heard of after 870, we can only speculate. Unfortunately, the end of his literary activities signifies the end of Eriugena. William of Malmesbury's account of his going to England during the reign of Alfred because of suspicions about his work could well be true, but William also records that Eriugena met his death in a rather bizarre fashion: his students stabbed him fatally with their pens.[7] There has been some scholarly debate as to whether this account of Eriugena's death is to be understood literally or figuratively. If we argue for the literal interpretation, we could say that given Eriugena's love of the Greek fathers and his inclusion of Greek themes in his work (and therefore, possibly also in his teaching), he may well have upset those holding more traditional views, especially in relation to thorny theological issues. The figurative interpretation rests on the idea that the dullness of his students' work literally killed, not only his spirit, but also his body! Some scholars believe that Eriugena was most likely confused with another Iohannes at Oxford at that time. Later accounts of his life were based on William's, and the embellishments of fifteenth- and sixteenth-century historians eventually led to the inclusion of "St. Ioannes Scotus" in the *Roman Martyrology* in 1586. Thus the "martyr" of Malmesbury was canonized (albeit briefly) six hundred years after he disappeared from contemporary records.[8]

Interestingly, one aspect of the Irishman's literary output has proven important in compiling a biography: the poetry he wrote has helped scholars date some events in his literary career.[9] Most poems relate to, or were written for, Charles the Bald, and many celebrate major Christian feasts. Some of the longer poems, such as *Aulae sidereae*, contain Neoplatonic themes and are important in understanding his work as a whole.

The Liberal Arts:
Eriugena as Teacher

It is most likely that Eriugena began his public life as a teacher of the liberal arts at the palace school of Charles, and contemporary accounts describe him as a learned and erudite man. References in his early treatise *On Predestination* suggest a close knowledge of secular learning in the trivium and quadrivium. As a teacher of the liberal arts, he would have relied heavily on the *Consolation of Philosophy* of Boethius and the *Marriage of Mercury and Philology* of Martianus Capella, the popular handbooks for secular learning at the time. Eriugena's own commentary on Martianus, the *Annotationes in Marcianum*, has generated some scholarly debate since Cora Lutz published the first edition in 1939, and to date the problems have not been resolved satisfactorily.[10] The confusion arises because of discrepancies between the Paris manuscript edited by Cora Lutz and a manuscript discovered at Oxford. A Leiden manuscript with Eriugenian glosses further complicates the issue. However, it has been suggested that the possible origin of these manuscripts as classroom notes may well account for the differences between them. Whatever the reason, it is most likely that over a period of time, Eriugena would have made extensive glosses on the work he used as a teaching tool. While he understood the importance of the liberal arts in general (his general definitions of the arts are given in *Periphyseon* I 475A–B), as the basis for a correct study and understanding of the scriptures they were indispensable. Eriugena firmly believed in the guiding principle: *nemo intrat in caelum nisi per philosophiam* (no one enters heaven unless through philosophy). Christian education should, as Augustine had stressed, study the ancient texts. Eriugena and the other ninth-century scholars followed in the tradition of Cassiodorus (*The Institutions of Divine and Human Readings*), where the liberal arts were understood as an *ancilla* (handmaid) to the study of the sacred texts. Therefore, there is no doubt that Eriugena's initial education had a firm foundation in secular learning. We could say that the earlier ambiguous attitude to classical authorities (exemplified by the famous question of Tertullian: "What has Athens to do with Jerusalem?") had finally been resolved, and a healthy attitude to all authorities, both secular and Christian, had set the stage for later education programs.

Eriugena as Translator

The wide range of Eriugena's translations from Greek into Latin was remarkable in his time: the complete works of the Pseudo-Dionysius, the *Quaestiones ad Thalassium* of Maximus the Confessor, the *De hominis opificio* of Gregory of Nyssa (which Eriugena called *De imagine*), and part of the *Ambigua ad Iohannes* of Maximus.[11] As a translator, Eriugena stood out in the ninth century because so few of his contemporaries could read Greek (in much the same way, few Greeks could read Latin). But of all the works he translated, the works of the Pseudo-Dionysius were to have the most influence in the history of Western thought. Around 860, Charles the Bald requested a new translation of the manuscript sent by the emperor of Constantinople, Michael the Stammerer, to Louis the Pious in 827, already translated by Hilduin, abbot of St. Denis between 832 and 835. The manuscript of the Dionysian works would have been regarded as a very precious gift (a previous manuscript had been sent by Paul I to Pippin the Short in 758), because Dionysius was understood to be the patron saint of Paris. Indeed, on the night when the manuscript Eriugena was to translate was received on the feast of St. Denis, several miraculous cures were reported at the abbey of St. Denis outside Paris. Chiefly through the translations of these works and the subsequent incorporation of their themes into his own work, Eriugena was responsible for the meeting of Athens and Rome in Gaul. Eriugena's translation of the Dionysian corpus begins the public life of this elusive theologian in the West (the earliest mention in the East was at a theological assembly in Constantinople in 532).

The Pseudo-Dionysius was most likely a Syrian monk of the late fifth century.[12] His works display the obvious influence of the late Neoplatonism of Proclus (410–85), but for whatever reason, the author assumed the identity of St. Paul's Athenian convert (Acts 17:22–34). Like Eriugena himself, this Dionysius remains an elusive figure, shrouded, most aptly in his case, in obscurity. Although the authority of Dionysius had been questioned by scholars in the intervening centuries, it was not until 1895, when two German scholars, Josef Stiglmayr and Hugo Koch, published (independently), articles that showed the unmistakable influence of late Neoplatonism, that Dionysius was revealed as "Pseudo." However, that discovery does not diminish the important influence that his works exerted on the philosophical and theological development of the medieval period when his authority was extremely highly regarded. Because Eriugena thought he was dealing with the writings of a first-century author, the works of Dionysius did not present him with the problems they still present for some readers today: are they representative of a truly Christian theology or are they simply a form of Neoplatonism in a Christian disguise? Scholarly opinion remains divided on this issue.

Eriugena attempted the translation of the complicated works of the Pseudo-Dionysius well aware of the difficulties involved in the task. He completed the work (as Hilduin had done before him and Sarrazin and Robert Grosseteste, among others, were to do after him),[13] and his translation shows a real capacity to understand this very obscure author; in fact, Dionysius himself claimed to be elucidating the obscure doctrines of his own teacher Hierotheus (*Divine Names*, III 2. 681B). While it is generally agreed that Eriugena's translation is sometimes deficient (Hilduin's is much more accurate in some instances), and at least once he deliberately mistranslates, many scholars believe that Eriugena's text exhibits a strong affinity with the ideas of the Pseudo-Dionysius and that his translation is close to the meaning of the Greek text.[14] He was concerned not only with the technical difficulty of putting Greek words into Latin (like Grosseteste after him, he also found it necessary to coin new words) but also with conveying the sense of the text, even though at times he gives the text an interpretation not originally intended. In other words, he was concerned with the spirit and not simply the letter of the text. Whether as a sign of arrogance or simply confidence in his own abilities, at the end of the translations he challenges his readers to check the accuracy of his translation against the original—a task that few in his time could have attempted.

What is important is that for Eriugena, translating the works of the Pseudo-Dionysius opened up a whole new world of ideas, ideas that were to be formative in the development of his own thought. Aside from the strong Proclean influence, the earlier fathers of the Eastern church also find an echo in the Pseudo-Dionysius, especially Gregory of Nyssa. The themes contained in the works of the Pseudo-Dionysius, which will later find a place in Eriugena's massive *summa* of reality, include the unknowable nature of God, the roles of negative and positive theology, the themes of procession and return and hierarchy, and the importance of the scriptures (for Dionysius, the scriptures had represented "sacred veils" around the divine). For Dionysius, the Augustinian concordance of true religion and true philosophy is expressed as philosophy being the same wisdom as that sought by St. Paul. Although there are many thematic similarities between the Pseudo-Dionysius and Eriugena, the focus of the two theologians was not the same, as I will show later. One further important work of Eriugena closely related to the Dionysian corpus is his *Commentary on the Celestial Hierarchy*, in which he sets out his own understanding of that important, difficult work.[15]

The Feather of the Peacock

In the *Periphyseon*, undoubtedly Eriugena's greatest work, we find him turning to many sources in the search for the truth of reality, but his fundamental source is the scriptures, one of the great Carolingian preoccupations. However, studying the sacred texts was not simply academic study like any other, for an intellectual understanding alone was not sufficient: as a foundation for a particular way of life, study of the scriptures meant that wisdom involved both intellectual and spiritual progress. Eriugena's own biblical glosses bear testimony to the importance of scriptural texts for scholarly pursuits in the ninth century.

For Eriugena, the relationship between the "book of nature" and the scriptures is infinite, just as "in one and the same feather of a peacock . . . we see a marvelously beautiful variety of innumerable colours" (P. IV 749C; II 560A). The four levels of the intelligible world of the scriptures correspond to the four interrelated levels of the sensible world: historical, literal, ethical, and theological (*Hom.* XIV 291B–C and P. V 1010B). The theological level is, of course, the supreme level of contemplation of the divine nature. However, for Eriugena, scriptural texts cannot be studied in isolation at whatever level; reason is an indispensable aid in determining the true meaning of the scared texts: "we must follow reason which investigates the truth of things" (P. I 509A), but the the scriptures remain the ultimate guide to truth (P. V 1010B–C). According to Eriugena's understanding, if reason and the sacred texts appear to come into conflict, that is because scripture uses allegories when speaking of God in order that the human mind can more easily understand divine reality from the things it knows (P. I 509A). Eriugena's continual warnings against believing the words of the scriptures only in their literal sense, demonstrates his scepticism about language, which ultimately results in his preference for negative theology. According to Bernard McGinn, "the sacred text contained a horizontal, or historical, pole of meaning, as well as a vertical, or mystico-theological one, both of which forbade any simplified, surface-level reading."[16] The authority of the scriptures "is not to be believed as a book which always uses verbs and nouns in their proper sense when it teaches us about the Divine Nature" (P. I 509A). Eriugena's prohibition here has recourse to the Pseudo-Dionysius, who also admonished that we should not say anything about God except that which has been revealed in the scriptures: "For as there is no place in which it is more proper to seek Thee than in Thy words, so there is no place where Thou art more clearly discovered than in Thy words" (P. V 1010C). "More clearly discovered than in Thy words"—this is not entirely true because the apparent conflict between reason and the scriptures is not the only conflict brought into focus by Eriugena. The sacred texts themselves contain many contradictory texts with which the exegete is forced to deal in the journey toward the truth about human and divine reality. In the *Periphyseon*, one of the most perplexing of these concerns the nature of the beatific vision, for not only do the authorities (Augustine and the Pseudo-Dionysius) come into conflict over this most difficult question, but contradictory texts in the scriptures themselves force the exegete to maneuver very skilfully in order to adjudicate among the various texts and interpretations. The scriptural conflict concerns I Corinthians 13:12 and I Timothy 6:16: shall we see God "face to face" or shall the inaccessible light of God be forever obscured to human intellects? This example of the confusing variations of color in the feather of the peacock (described by Tom O'Loughlin as an *antikeimenon,* after the collection of *Antikeimenon* of Julian of Toledo)[17] is one of the many conflicts Eriugena confronts in his writings, and I discuss this particular point in chapter 7. It is in "solving" such conflicts that his exegetical skills can be appreciated as both diplomatic and respectful. Of course, Eriugena does not struggle alone in the search for a correct understanding of the texts of the scriptures: he enlists the support of the fathers, many of whom had already grappled with the same questions. According to Contreni, Carolingian commentators "plucked flowers from fields to compose a rich bouquet. . . . In the process they defined a new kind of exegesis," one that concentrated on the texts themselves as complementary to the authority of the fathers.[18]

The study of the scriptures in the quest for spiritual meaning, therefore, is guided not only by the authority of the fathers but also by reason, which "finds it sweeter to exercise her skill in the hidden straits of the ocean of divinity than idly to bask in smooth and open waters where she cannot display her power" (P. IV 744A). Eriugena conveys a sense of the excitement about the journey to be undertaken through the vast seas of the scriptures, and we are never in any doubt that his ship will reach a safe harbor because reason acts as his guide—precisely what Hincmar and Prudentius complained about in the predestination treatise. Eriugena's own exegesis, characterized by his ship of reason steering its way through dangerous and stormy seas, often delights the reader with his choice of texts and interpretations. However, the toil of human reason to come to a correct understanding of the sacred texts has been made more difficult because of the damage sustained by reason through the fall. Through the transgression of Adam and Eve, reason must work doubly hard, through sorrow and hard labor, to come to a proper understanding of all that is related in the book of the scriptures and in the book of nature (P. IV 855A–B).

Of all the scriptural texts on which Eriugena comments, the *Homily on the Prologue of John* and *Commentary on the Gospel of John* show that John the Evangelist obviously had a special significance for him.[19] It is in these works that we see the more spiritual nature of Eriugena's exegesis. The solitary eagle, whose eye can see the whole of reality from its vantage point in the sky, is John, whose feathers of theology allowed him, like Moses, to enter into the secrets of the divine mysteries (*Hom.* V 285D; IX 288A). In chapter 7 I argue that Eriugena's preference for John over Moses is indicative of his remodeling of the account of the spiritual journey to be found in Gregory of Nyssa and the Pseudo-Dionysius. While we can discern the influence of many of the great fathers of the preceding centuries in Eriugena's own works, he was no slavish follower of the ideas of others: the mark of his own exegetical genius is evident throughout the *Periphyseon*, as I will show later.

Authorities

Part of Eriugena's appeal is that he cannot be categorized easily as of the school of Augustine or as a follower of the Pseudo-Dionysius, although he is very much a product of all he read and assimilated from the fathers of both East and West.[20] Eriugena's genius at work is revealed in his mastery of many authorities, both secular and Christian, a feat that can perhaps be paralleled by Aquinas's similar talent in terms of his vast knowledge of Greek, Latin, Jewish, and Arabic thought. One very important point to be made regarding Eriugena's Latin sources is that most, if not all, of the Latin Christian authors he had read transmitted a Platonic or Neoplatonic outlook. The influence of Aristotle on Eriugena was secondary in nature and was transmitted through the Pseudo-Augustinian *On the Ten Categories*, the *Isagoge* of Porphyry (paraphrased in Latin by Marius Victorinus), the translations of Boethius of the logical works of Aristotle, and Boethius's own commentaries on Aristotle (which did aim at a reconciliation of Plato and Aristotle). The influence of Aristotle is also discernible through Maximus the Confessor, whom Eriugena had read and translated. Other secular authors mentioned in his works include Virgil, Pliny, Ptolemy, and Macrobius's commentary on the *Dream of Scipio* (an extract from Cicero's *Republic* dealing with the Platonic doctrine of soul).

On the Christian side, Eriugena had read the Western fathers Ambrose of Milan, Augustine, Hilary, Isidore, Jerome, and Gregory the Great, but Augustine was by far the Latin authority he relied on most. More than forty years ago, Étienne Gilson noted that the influence of Augustine in the works of Eriugena was exaggerated; more recent work has shown that he does, in fact, achieve a certain balance in his reliance on both Eastern and Western authorities.[21] Gilson's observation that Eriugena wrote in Latin but thought in Greek can be challenged by recognizing the specific influence of Augustine on Eriugena, which has been the focus of much scholarly research, although in the context of this work it would be too long a task to enumerate the many debts Eriugena held with Augustine. To stretch the analogy a little, it would be like asking what Plotinus took from Plato: the answer is much but remodeled.[22] Augustine's shadow falls squarely over Eriugena but does not hold him captive. Although Eriugena's Augustinian background can be seen clearly throughout his works, perhaps Eriugena's most fundamental and unspoken identification with Augustine lies in his dogged pursuit of truth and his consuming desire for divine wisdom; "there is no worse death than ignorance of the truth" (P. III 650A). One aspect of Eriugena's reliance on Augustine is that the latter was an important source of Neoplatonic principles; Augustine would undoubtedly have been Eriugena's primary contact with the Neoplatonism of Plotinus and Porphyry. This initial influence of Neoplatonism would have been strengthened by the later influence of Proclus through the Pseudo-Dionysius. While the more Plotinian form of Neoplatonism present in the works of Gregory of Nyssa and Basil of Caesarea would not have been unfamiliar to Eriugena, the focus would have been different from that of Augustine.

The Cappadocian Fathers—Gregory of Nyssa and Gregory Nazianzus (whom Eriugena confuses at times), as well as Maximus the Confessor—can be said to have been the formative Greek influences on Eriugena. Maximus was especially important because of his remodeling and interpretation of the Dionysian corpus. Eriugena's translation of Gregory of Nyssa's *On the Making of Man* (*De imagine*) was obviously a formative influence on him; large portions of this work are identifiable and indeed are quoted in the *Periphyseon.* Apart from Maximus and the Cappadocian Fathers, Eriugena had also read some works of Basil of Caeserea and Epiphanius (though whom he encountered Origen). Of course, Greek influence would also have filtered through to Eriugena through his reading of the works of Ambrose and Hilary, both of whom knew Greek and incorporated Greek themes and ideas in their own works.[23]

It has often been stated that what we find in Eriugena's work is a constant battle between Augustine and the Pseudo-Dionysius, broadly understood as West versus East.[24] While that characterization is not entirely false, it could be said that Eriugena was simply trying to bring the diverse strands of Christian theology into agreement, perhaps even more subconsciously than we would imagine. However, it would be misleading to suggest that Eriugena achieved a smooth confluence of Eastern and Western sources while favoring the Greeks over the Latins in many instances of dispute. The danger here, as Willemien Otten points out, is that we could evaluate the *Periphyseon* "as a Greek interruption in what is consequently characterized as an ongoing Latin tradition."[25] Eriugena often takes the side of a Greek father in preference to the authority of Augustine, and at times not without what some scholars would regard as a slight on Augustine. Even though Eriugena may have understood the authority of Augustine in much the same light as he regarded the authority of the scriptures, that is, capable of many readings, at times he takes tremendous liberties with Augustinian texts, and he sometimes misinterprets Augustine with the aim of bringing his thought into line with the great Eastern authorities (sometimes Eriugena says that Augustine does not mean what he says). In this sense, Eriugena does not abide by his self-imposed stricture not to adjudicate between the fathers but to acknowledge their views with piety and reverence and select that which most accords with the meaning of the scriptures (P. II 548D; IV 814A–B, 816D–817A, 829A–B). He also notes that the opinions of the fathers can be especially helpful for those untrained in reason and more amenable to authority (P. IV 781C–D). Even though true authorities come from the same source, the wisdom of God (P. II 511B), conflict can still arise. Interestingly, when Eriugena finds disagreement between authorities, he is generally anxious to explain the reason. For example, with regard to Basil of Caeserea's view that the soul of animals die with the death of their bodies (not a view he will subscribe to), Eriugena explains that Basil simply meant to illustrate for simple people the fact that a base life can lead to the loss of soul (P. III 736B–739C).

It is, however, still generally believed that despite the very powerful and formative influence of Augustine, Eriugena was more Greek than Latin in his approach to created reality and its relationship with divine reality. The Greek coloring of Eriugena's thought, however, is not simply a veneer on a Latin base coat: Eriugena genuinely sided with the Greek fathers on many important issues. According to John Meyendorff, Eriugena "did not use Greek patristic authors simply to find prooftexts; he did understand and adopt for himself the logic of Christian Neoplatonism."[26] Eriugena's anthropology, more specifically his conception of the whole of humanity as in the image of God eventually to be restored to its divine exemplar, is more obviously Greek than Latin in its theocentric character. The concept of deification (of human being becoming God), which Eriugena notes is more difficult for the Latins (with the exception of Ambrose), is a very powerful Greek thematic in the *Periphyseon*, which he tries to reconcile with Latin authorities on the subject. Eriugena's importance in terms of his knowledge of the Greek fathers meant that the estrangement between Greek East and Latin West was slightly lessened in the ninth century. While we could hardly describe ninth-century thought as straitjacketed, the very powerful and immediate presence of the Greek fathers constituted a different perspective in terms of the Latin theology Eriugena had inherited from Augustine. In conclusion, while one can say that while Eriugena was constantly working to bring his various sources into agreement, one must also remember that for him all authority was human authority and must, therefore, conform to reason.

The *Periphyseon*

The *Periphyseon*, Eriugena's greatest, most original work, which was begun around 864, can be said to represent the culmination of his thought and teaching. Dedicated to Wulfad, Abbot of St. Médard and tutor to Charles the Bald's son Carlomannus, the work takes the form of a dialogue between the *nutritor* (master) and the *alumnus* (disciple). This literary device introduces a very human element into a difficult work. At times the alumnus is confused, shocked, surprised, bored, restless, or doggedly questioning the nutritor until the point of discussion has been clarified to his satisfaction.

However, despite the now recognized greatness of the work, the *Periphyseon* was to have a rather checkered history (Eriugena's own sense of foreboding evident in the final pages of the *Periphyseon* [V 1021D–1022C] was to prove correct): it was included in the condemnations of 1050, 1059, 1210, and 1225. The first printing of the *Periphyseon* was made at Oxford by Thomas Gale in 1681, and it was placed on the *Index of Prohibited Books* three years later in 1684. The reasons for its less than enthusiastic reception will become clear as I explain Eriugena's ideas in the present work. The edition of Henricus-Josephus Floss in the *Patrologia Latina* (volume 122), published in 1865, has finally been replaced by a new edition in the *Scriptores Latini Hiberniae* series. Inglis P. Sheldon-Williams edited the first three volumes (1968, 1972, and 1981). Édouard Jeauneau has undertaken the edition of the final two volumes, the first of which was published in 1995. Volume V is still in preparation.[27]

The *Periphyseon* consists of five books, although according to Jeauneau, Eriugena originally planned four books to correspond to the four divisions of nature which form the plan and substructure of the work.[28] Book I outlines the five modes of being and non-being, introduces the four divisions of nature, and examines the first division of nature: the role of God as uncreated creator. There is a lengthy excursus on negative theology and discussions on the nature of the Trinity, theophany, and the applicability of the ten categories to the divine nature. Book II examines the second division of nature in relation to how procession through the primordial causes is the source of diversity in the visible world. Here Eriugena also discusses the concept of divine ignorance and the original creation of human beings and again broaches a discussion of the nature of the Trinity. Book III concludes the discussion of the primordial causes and introduces the examination of the third division of nature, created effects, through lengthy discussions on participation and nothing. A hexaemeral commentary (on the six days of creation in Genesis) concludes book III and ends on the fifth day of creation. Eriugena describes the first three books using the image of steering a ship through the smooth seas of the scriptures, copiloted on many occasions by the great fathers of both East and West: "the first three books seem like a smooth sea upon which, because of the calmness of the waves, readers could sail without fear of shipwreck, steering a safe course" (P. IV 743C–744A). Books IV and V enter more dangerous seas, characterized by the heavy currents and concealed rocks of obscure and conflicting doctrines. Eriugena is sure of surviving, however, not simply because his course has already been charted by the navigations of Augustine, Ambrose and Gregory of Nyssa, among others, but also because his ship of exegesis is guided by reason (P. IV 744A). Book IV, which Eriugena himself notes is more difficult than preceding books, begins with an interpretation of the sixth day of creation and is a treatise on human nature. Book V, the longest book in the *Periphyseon*, deals chiefly with the process of *reditus*, the return of all created things to their source (which is God, the uncreated uncreating), and the nature of the theophanies that await when finally God shall be "all in all" (1 Cor. 15:28).

Although the *Periphyseon* promises a structured development and a logical discussion of the four divisions of *physis*, this promise is not fulfilled, as Eriugena digresses repeatedly in order to clarify difficult points. As a result, the *Periphyseon* is not a neat, tidy work; rather, it gives the impression of being work in progress. At times, Eriugena tries his reader's patience, and his frequent digressions and repetitions often seem unnecessary to the modern reader—and as Jeauneau notes, perhaps also to his ninth-century reader.[29] Eriugena sounds an interesting note of warning in book II when the alumnus becomes impatient with the "digressions" on human nature. He is told that if he seeks to find the solution by himself, he will surpass his own powers of reasoning: "[f]or if it is found it is not he who searches but He who is sought and who is the Light of our minds Who finds it" (P. II 572A–B). However, the digressions, cul-de-sacs, strange pathways, and unexpected diversions in the *Periphyseon* are full of surprises that can delight, shock, and provoke.

Although Eriugena's Neoplatonism is strikingly evident in the *Periphyseon*, his main theme is creation: the process by which the unmanifest God becomes visible and its ultimate return to its source. How *divisio* and *resolutio* can be said to characterize the entire work is through the application of the art of dialectic. Dialectic, "the science of good disputation" (P. V 869A) is Eriugena's preferred method of explication precisely because it is the method of the creative process at work (as is made explicit in Gen. 1:24) and its ultimate return to unity. According to Eriugena, dialectic, which divides and resolves into unity, "did not arise from human contrivances, but was first implanted in nature by the originator of all the arts" (P. IV 749A).

The *Periphyseon* is a spirited attempt to provide not an alternative view of reality (although it certainly does that, especially for those more familiar with the teaching of the traditionally more mainstream thinkers of the medieval period) but rather a refreshing enquiry into the whole of *natura* from Eriugena's own unique perspective. Eriugena's greatness was not that he transcended the limits of ninth-century philosophy (in that he has been understood to prefigure some more recent philosophers) but that his dialectical and open understanding of the nature of reality injected the exciting elements of Eastern thought and secular learning into the artery of a burgeoning intellectualism. The ideas he drew on from the great Eastern fathers opened a new window onto a fresh understanding of human and divine reality. It remains true that we still view the *Periphyseon* as an innovative work for the simple reason that few Western thinkers have dared to conceive of a metaphysical or theological analysis of reality that combines elements of both East and West. Although

Eriugena's reflections were developed against a different philosophical and theological background, the ideas elaborated in the *Periphyseon* can be understood as a very powerful alternative to the views elaborated by Augustine and later by Aquinas. That is, I believe, where the appeal of the *Periphyseon* lies, especially for the contemporary reader. The central idea that creation is the manifestation of God and, therefore, is sanctified, since all things have come from the same source, is very much in vogue in some theological thinking today. Eriugena's preference for a more dynamic understanding of the unfolding of natura over against the more traditional understanding of cause and effect, of creator and creation as having strictly demarcated boundaries, is one of the most interesting underlying themes in the *Periphyseon*. However, the *Periphyseon* is not an easy work to categorize: "in the context of one and the same work we find a philosophical debate on the categories intertwined with a theological discussion of the divine names which changes next into discourse of historical, and even allegorical exegesis."[30]

Eriugena approaches the subject of natura with evident enthusiasm and excitement while never forgetting the importance of illustrations, especially from the natural world. The whole work is characterized by meticulous scriptural exegesis, and Eriugena leaves few stones unturned in the attempt to reach the truth. His keenness of mind, sharpened through the literary device of the nutritor and the alumnus in animated discussion with one another, is an original attempt to tackle many difficult subjects and to dispel the clouds of darkness in order to arrive at sure knowledge, for there is no worse death than ignorance of the truth (P. III 650A). Throughout the entire work Eriugena displays his erudition and his knowledge of the natural world: cosmology, physics, astronomy, number theory (which is especially important in his exegesis of the six first days of creation), and music serve him in good stead as he attempts to explain natura and all that can be understood about human and divine reality. The image of the *penna pavonis*, the "feather of the peacock" (P. IV 749C), is a very apt way to describe the *Periphyseon* itself: the wonderful variety of colors represents the wonderful variety of themes in Eriugena's work. Book I, however, is a book of muted colors, despite the important discussions it contains, and it leaves the reader with the impression that Eriugena was simply a metaphysician, albeit an innovative one, with apophatic leanings; nothing could be further from the truth, as further reading demonstrates. The scope of ideas and themes discussed by Eriugena is, at least to my mind, comparable to the *Enneads* of Plotinus in terms of richness and food for sustained thought. Eriugena's fascination with the beauty, harmony, and intricate workings of the universe (culminating in the creation of human nature in the image of God), which is an ineffable unity held in being by the Word, is, to my mind, the one characteristic of the *Periphyseon* that leaves a lasting impression with the reader long after particular details of philosophical of theological importance have been forgotten. The *Periphyseon*, with all its digressions

PART II • THE WAY DOWN

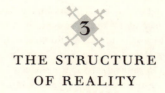

THE STRUCTURE
OF REALITY

Eriugena's overall view of reality, both human and divine, will be familiar to students of Neoplatonism, based as it is on the dual movement of procession and return: every effect remains in its cause, proceeds from it, and returns to it.[1] Although I have chosen to discuss Eriugena's ideas within the framework of *divisoria* and *resolutiva* (*diairetike* and *analytike*), both "ways" must be understood as intrinsically entwined and, strictly speaking, are not separate movements or processes. "For the procession of the creatures and the return of the same are so intimately associated in the reason which considers them that they appear to be inseparable the one from the other" (P. II 529A, 532A). As I will show, the link between the two is the Word: divisoria is through the Word, and the Word is also the first principle of resolutiva. Eriugena's method begins with the mind's dialectical process of breaking down a concept or problem into its constituent parts and then reassembling it. The science of dialectics, which had been outlined in the treatise *On Predestination* as division, definition, demonstration, and resolution, in the *Periphyseon* concentrates on division and resolution. Dialectic, as the "mother of the arts," can descend from genus to species or ascend from species to genus (P. V 870B). According to Paul Rorem, Eriugena applied this method to the "macrocosm of metaphysics" in that he adapted the Neoplatonic theme of *exitus* and *reditus* "to the entire history of God and the world."[2]

The dialectical method that Eriugena elaborates through exitus and reditus operates both on an epistemological level (the way the human mind operates) and on an ontological level (the way reality is structured). In fact, there is an interlocking relationship in Eriugena's thought between reality and how the human mind structures reality. The vast project of mapping out the contours of natura in the *Periphyseon* is based on the human mind's control of the linear or circular unfolding of natura and its ultimate resolution in its source.

Human rationality and the limitations of the mind become the determinants of, and set the boundaries for, natura, as I will show in chapter 5. The starting point of the *Periphyseon* is natura (physis) taken in all its inclusiveness: "all things which are and which are not," both being and non-being (P. I 441A). This initial division, *quae sunt et quae non sunt*, the source of which can be traced to Marius Victorinus, the famous Roman orator, Boethius, and the Pseudo-Dionysius, is a phrase Eriugena uses not only in the *Periphyseon* but also in the treatise *On Predestination* and the *Homilia*.[3] According to reason, "nothing at all can come into our thought that would not fall under this term" (P. I 441A); indeed, as I will show, things both within and outside the mind's grasp are included in the genus natura. In this sense, the mind serves as the determination of natura, which comprises both the finite and the infinite—a bold step on Eriugena's part, given the existing philosophical and theological trends of his time. The basic difference between being and non-being, which is based solely on the capabilities of the human mind, means that Eriugena's cosmology is based on human insight, truly a daring and innovative thesis to defend.[4] On Eriugena's part, the use of the all-inclusive term *natura* can be seen as an attempt to explain a totally rational, logically divided universe.[5] However, despite Eriugena's efforts to find a comprehensive category through which to explain reality, human rationality itself, in the process of determining that which is and that which is not, is confronted with its own limitations, which, as I will show in chapter 6, stem from the fall. Natura, which includes non-being, necessarily escapes finite boundaries and cannot be defined fully. Nevertheless Eriugena, at the helm of the good ship Reason, enters into uncharted waters with a daring and fearless spirit. Whether or not he succeeds in this mammoth task will become clearer as I examine the structure of natura as it is presented in the *Periphyseon*.

Division and Resolution

Book I of the *Periphyseon* finds the nutritor and the alumnus engaged in a discussion of how the genus natura can be understood. The four divisions or species that are derived from this genus through the process of diairetike show the Christian focus of universal nature: that which creates and is not created; that which is created and creates; that which is created and does not create; and that which is not created and does not create (P. I 441B). The first division denotes God as cause; the second division refers to the causes of all things created by God in the Word; the third division denotes all that is created by the causes; the fourth division refers to God as end. The source of this division of natura has been the topic of much scholarly discussion and Bede, Marius Victorinus, Boethius, Augustine, and Pythagorean number theory have been among the sources suggested.[6] While scholarly detective work has uncovered a number of likely sources for Eriugena's divisions, I believe Pythagorean number theory to be the most likely because of a rather explicit passage in the writings of Philo of Alexandria that reflects the division of natura as outlined by Eriugena: some numbers beget without being begotten; some beget and are begotten; some are begotten without begetting; and one neither begets nor is begotten (*On the Making of the World* 99–100). While further investigation on this particular theme could perhaps be undertaken, the similarity between the text in Philo and the divisions as explained by Eriugena is such that it is likely that Eriugena's entire scheme may have derived from a Pythagorean source, whether or not from Philo through Origen. The fourth division, that which is not created and does not create, which is an important logical component in the jigsaw of natura as envisaged by Eriugena, has been the focus of some debate, not only in terms of its source but also because it can be "classed among the impossibles" (P. I 442A). If it neither creates nor is created, then logically it cannot be. However, Eriugena's way of thinking about and expressing the mystery at the heart of all reality is not confined to the logic of language, although it is constrained by the limits of rationality. As I will show, the concept of the non-being of God as the ground of being constantly puts a strain on all formulated concepts in the sense that meaning and knowledge are reassigned to a very precarious position. Otten's portrayal of human reason operating "on the verge of complete confusion" because its grasp of reality is slim as a result of the fall is an accurate description of the mind's position. In Otten's view, the principle of rationality is constantly under stress as reason attempts to clarify the totality of natura, which is necessarily beyond the mind's capabilities.[7] The tension between the divisions of natura, between creator and created, serve to heighten further the difficulties involved in mapping out the details of natura. Despite the mind's division of natura into the four parts, they remain parts of one whole, although two create and two do not create. Eriugena explains that the first and third divisions are opposites and the second and fourth divisions are opposites (P. I 442A; II 525C–526A). The opposition is finally resolved, but only after Eriugena has fleshed out each aspect of this division with precision, and it must be said, with a great deal of ingenuity.

One very important question, perhaps the most important question in relation to this particular issue, raised by the alumnus early in book III of the *Periphyseon*, concerns the reason why God, who is unbounded and infinite, is included as the first part of the universe, which is necessarily bounded by limit and finitude (620B–621A). The nutritor answers that God is not placed among the divisions of the created universe but among the divisions of that universe which is denoted by the term natura. This understanding of natura includes not only the created universe but also its creator; both together signify universal nature. However, there is some ambiguity in the *Periphyseon* with regard to the use of the term natura, and Eriugena is not consistent in using it to denote both the finite and the infinite; sometimes it is used to refer only to created realities.[8]

A further articulation of the divisions of reality, and a frequently repeated formula in the *Periphyseon,* is that God is the beginning, middle, and end of the created universe. God is that from which all things originate, that in which all things participate, and that to which all things will eventually return (P. III 621A–622A). As beginning and end, God can be understood in terms of the first and fourth divisions; as middle, we are to understand all created nature: the causes and the effects of those causes. Eriugena illustrates this conception of God as the source of all division and the end of all resolution using the example of the monad (the number one) as the source of all numbers; the center of the circle, the sign of the figure, and the point of the line can be understood in similar fashion (P. III 621C–D). The fact that God can be understood as all three is, Eriugena explains, the result of the triple movement of theological *theoria* (P. III 688B–C); these three cannot, of course, be distinguished in God. Human minds understand God according to different perspectives because of their finite, human-bound understanding. Similarly, the apparent duality of all natura is the result of deficient human understanding. The dual aspect observed in the first and last species of natura is a human construction in the mind, while the second and third divisions are to be understood both in the mind and in reality (P. II 528A). Division (and ultimate resolution) is simply an attempt of the human mind to impose some degree of comprehensibility on the concept natura. Our "double contemplation" sees God only in relation to created reality, which has a beginning and an end, and thus it makes a distinction in relation to God's nature. In contemplating natura in its comprehensiveness, the human mind, through divisoria and resolutiva, echoes the rhythm of creation itself, which is in eternal movement from unity back to unity.

With the process of divisoria explained to the satisfaction of the alumnus, the nutritor takes up the important themes of the nature of divine manifestation (theophany) and negative theology, and the remainder of book I is taken up with an examination of the categories as they relate to the divine essence. This exercise is not simply a logical one but provides the key to an understanding of how to interpret all that will be said about God in the books to follow. In book II, which opens with a summary of the divisions of natura, the nutritor finally explains how all division can ultimately be resolved. In God, there can be no duality; beginning and end have no temporal reality but are simultaneous and can, therefore, be reduced to a unity (P. II 527B). In the same way, the second and third divisions can be understood simply as created reality. Thus, four become two: God and creation. Eriugena makes one further bold step in relation to the process of resolutiva: "[b]ut suppose you join the creature to the creator so as to understand that there is nothing in the former save Him who alone truly is . . . will you deny that Creator and creature are one?" (P. II 528B). The alumnus answers quite comfortably in the negative and admits that all natura can be reduced to "an indivisible One, being Principle as well as Cause and End" (P. II 528B). Surely this idea must be the reason why the *Periphyseon* was associated with pantheism? According to Eriugena's mind, the rationale for this assertion is that nothing apart from God truly is, for all things participate in God, indeed do not have being apart from God. The whole of reality, then, is God since God is source, sustainer, and end. This discussion, the far-reaching conclusion of which almost sneaks up on the alumnus without causing alarm or protestation, is almost rudely abandoned as the alumnus changes the subject to a discussion of the second division of natura; the nutritor develops the idea that God is all things later in books II and III.

However, I should point out here that despite the reduction of two divisions to one, Eriugena always retains a basic distinction between the self-manifestation of God (theophany) and God (in God's self). Even in final theophany, when all things will have returned to God and God shall be "all in all," Eriugena never "conflates" God and creature. The resolution of four divisions to two and two divisions to one accounts for the relationship between the divisions of universal natura, but does not explain away the uncreated aspect of God's nature, which has its source in divine reality, not in human conceptions of divine reality. Although the term "uncreated" is an integral part of the whole of natura as expressed in the *Periphyseon*, we cannot think that natura, however universal, somehow encapsulates the whole of God's infinite nature. Uncreated reality, which Eriugena expresses as "not being," is beyond both being and non-being, and no verbal account, no matter how well constructed, can take account of the infinite, which necessarily escapes the "whatness" of definition and limit. The final resolution of the four divisions of natura to one can indeed be said to "unite" the finite and the infinite but only in so far as that which is infinite refers to God's self-manifestation in theophany. The final dialectic operative in Eriugena's thought is that while God can be understood as part of universal natura, the infinite nature of the divine essence can only be hinted at, never grasped. God remains transcendently above all things.

> There is no one of those who devoutly believe and understand the truth who would not persistently and without any hesitation declare that the creative Cause of the whole universe is beyond nature and beyond being and beyond life and wisdom and power and beyond all things which are said and understood and perceived by any sense. (P. III 621D–622A)

Therefore, the concept of natura is not defined by Eriugena: it escapes the realm of definition precisely because the mind cannot grasp that which is designated non-being. As I will show, for Eriugena, non-being has primacy over being because non-being means more than being: "for being is from Him but He is not Himself being. For above this being after some manner there is More-than-being, and absolute Being beyond language and understanding" (P. I 482B; V 898A–C). In the same way we can argue that the transcendence of God has primacy over natura, and a correct interpretation of the resolution of the divisions discovered in natura must be understood in terms of the dialectical method Eriugena employs in the *Periphyseon*.

A Theocentric Universe:
Unity in Diversity

Eriugena's dialectical approach to the terms "creator" and "created" provides the focus for some interesting discussion in relation to causality in the *Periphyseon*. According to our commonly accepted understanding, we understand "creator" and "created" as two separate entities. Eriugena presents us with a wonderfully different slant on this familiar understanding. Strictly speaking, God is uncreated, yet in the act of creating, God creates God's self (*a se ipso creatur*). This means that God, as cause, is the essence of all things (P. I 454A); outside of God there is nothing (P. I 452C). Therefore, the second and third divisions of nature are eternal, since they are God, and they are made, since they are not God. But how can that which is one thing be another different thing? Such a contradiction cannot be reconciled unless we do away with temporal categories. How does Eriugena arrive at this conclusion?

The simultaneous timeless and time-bound character of creation depends on the fact that all things were created in the Word (as I will show in chapter 4) by God at the same time because God could not have existed before God created, a dim hint of Eckhart's audacious statement: "without me God would not be God" (see the vernacular sermon *Beati pauperes spiritu*). The procession of God into created effects means that all things have the one primordial cause, all things have the same beginning, and ultimately, all will have the same end. All things are, therefore, bound together in the unity of their cause: "the beauty of the whole established universe consists of a marvellous harmony of like and unlike . . . an ineffable unity" (P. III 638A). This unity is not a synthesis resulting from strict logical thought processes whereby Eriugena can "resolve" the four divisions of nature into one, but is a unity that already pervades all diversity and difference. What does Eriugena mean by these strange statements that, as the alumnus notes, have the power to bewilder and strike us dumb with wonder? (P. III 646C). What Eriugena means can be said to sum up the central metaphysical foundation of the *Periphyseon*, which can be painted in very broad strokes as follows. God can be understood as darkness because of God's transcendence, yet this darkness is really *lux excel-*

lentiam, an ineffable light that simply appears dark precisely because of its transcendent intensity (*Hom.* XIV 291B).[9] However, Eriugena's use of this Dionysian theme is not consistent in the *Periphyseon,* and as I have argued elsewhere, his employment of "la métaphysique nocturne" displays a certain ambiguity.[10] In the process of the going forth from God, the nothingness from which all things are created is actually God's self because there can be nothing coeternal and coexisting with God. This nothing becomes something through the creative process in that the unknowable reveals itself through creation and in so doing becomes something that both itself and created effects can know. The paradox of creation is that the original darkness of God, which is no thing, becomes light, becomes some thing. God's fullness above being is the "nothing" that is the negation of something, but through its becoming, it becomes the negation of the negation: the divine nature becomes "other" than itself: God becomes not-God through the process of *ex-stasis,* literally, God's *going out from* God.

Creation, then, according to the ideas elucidated primarily in the *Periphyseon,* simply means God's movement from nothing into being: from God into God. The transition from nothingness into something, indeed into all things, is "self-negation," but there is, paradoxically, no "self" to negate until the movement into the causes begins: "for as yet there is no essence" (P. III 683A). "For if the understanding of all things is all things and It alone understands all things, then It alone is all things. . . . For It encircles all things and there is nothing within It but what, in so far as it is, is not Itself, for It alone truly is" (P. III 632D–633A). Creation, therefore, does not refer to the making of things that exist outside of God, because in the very act of creating, the divine essence actually creates itself. "So it is from Himself that God takes the occasions of His theophanies, that is, of the divine apparitions, since all things are from Him and through Him and in Him and for Him" (P. III 679A). Thus it is that Eriugena can assert, quite confidently, that outside of God there is nothing (P. I 452C). "And while it is eternal it does not cease to be made, and made it does not cease to be eternal, and out of itself it makes itself, for it does not require some other matter which is not itself in which to make itself" (P. III 678D–679A). The act of creation is coeternal with God and coessential because Eriugena, in correct theological fashion, cannot compromise God's simplicity and infinity by acknowledging that God existed before God created.

The *processio* into created effects can be understood as an increasing lightening or brightening of being. A simple analogy can be helpful in explaining this point. When I walk into a dark room with which I am familiar (that is, I know that there are objects in the room) and turn on a dimmer switch, the room becomes progressively brighter and its contents can clearly be seen. Similarly, the emergence of God from transcendent darkness means that God can be seen, signified by the *fiat lux* of Genesis, in created effects. It is in this sense that the *lux trina,* in becoming brighter, in becoming "other" than itself, is the dialectical self-revelation of God. The darkness that is ineffable light becomes light in the darkness so that the light can return once again to the darkness. Thus, the process of creation is theophany—the appearance of God as other than God, the brightening of God—while at the same time God remains other than not God. God goes out to become not God, to become creature while remaining God, that is, God-in-otherness.[11] In the return, the complementary movement occurs: the creature goes out to become not creature, to become God while still remaining creature. Paradoxically, in the descent of God as other, God remains not other, and God is known both by God's self through what God has become and also by what God has become:

> the Divine Nature . . . allows itself to appear in its theophanies, willing to emerge from the most hidden recesses of its nature in which it is unknown even to itself, that is, knows itself in nothing because it is infinite and supernatural and superessential and beyond everything that can and cannot be understood; but by descending into the principles of things and, as it were, creating itself, it begins to know itself in something. (P. III 689B)

All being, therefore, is from God and in God and is God, while God remains transcendently not being or more than being (P. I 482B).

> Therefore descending first from the superessentiality of His Nature, in which He is said not to be, He is created by Himself in the primordial causes and becomes the beginning of all essence, of all life, of all intelligence . . . and thus going forth into all things in order He makes all things and is made in all things, and returns into Himself. (P. III 683A–B and *Hom.* XI 289B)

Circles have traditionally been an important image for a very practical understanding of much Neoplatonist thought, not least because a circle has neither definite beginning nor end. In a very basic sense, the movement from God and the return to God, both at the individual and cosmic levels, is neatly illustrated as circular movement. In similar terms, the creative activity of God can be described as follows. Imagine a series of circles, one behind the other, getting progressively smaller until only a point remains. No matter how small the point is, it can still be conceived of as the smallest possible circle, yet it remains a point to the naked eye. The converse movement can also be described as a point or infinitely small circle magnified or widening out into a series of circles increasing in size. The circular movement of *exitus* and *reditus* can be imagined as a spiraling process through creation (to the largest circle) and back again to its source. In this sense, Eriugena's thought shows its real Neoplatonic character: while remaining above all things or apart from all things (the center of the circle or the point), God moves into all things and truly becomes the essence of all things.

While one aspect of Eriugena's thought can be understood as an elucidation of the process of resolutiva when God shall be "all in all," the fact that things exist means that God is, in an ineffable way, already "all in all," although this is more difficult to appreciate from an earth-bound perspective. God cannot be understood as either "this" or "that," yet God is precisely "this and that" (P. I 468B). God is both the maker of all things and is made in all things (P. I 454C; III 650C–D), a very definite confusion of the laws of causality. "But if the creature [is] from God, God will be the Cause, but the creature the effect. But if an effect is nothing else but a made cause, it follows that God the Cause is made in His effects" (P. III 687C). According to Otten, this passage represents an inversion of the hierarchical order of cause and effect. "Instead of God creating the world in his capacity of being its eternal cause, it is God who becomes created through his effects. Eriugena thus appears completely to overturn the logical order of events as he comes to make creation almost responsible for God's unfolding as its cause."[12] Thus, it is the notion of theophany (the appearance of God) that guides Eriugena's confident and repeated assertion that God is all things.

The continuous dialectic in Eriugena's thought must be understood not only in the context of his understanding of divine reality from the viewpoint of negative theology, but also in terms of the metaphysical foundations of his thought. That God is all things is a very basic Neoplatonic, specifically Plotinian, assertion (*to hen panta*), which sees all multiplicity as an underlying unity, and yet the One is not all things simply because it is the One (*Enn.* VI 7, 32, 12–40). That God is all things and yet is not all things, is both transcendent and immanent, is the theological equivalent of the philosophical assertion of unity in diversity. The whole of natura is a basic unity characterized by diversity and difference. In the act of creation, which Eriugena often describes as a flowing out from or diffusion from God, things remain in their cause and will ultimately return to it.

> For the whole river first flows forth from its source, and through its channel the water which first wells up in the source continues to flow always without any break to whatever distance it extends. So the Divine Goodness and Essence . . . first flow down into the primordial causes . . . flowing forth continuously through the higher to the lower; and return back again to their source. (P. III 632B–C)

However, the basic concept that Eriugena describes in the *Periphyseon*, God is all things (God appears in created effects), is constantly thwarted by the affirmation of the dialectical truth of God's concealment in God's self in the darkness of inaccessible light. In this sense Eriugena's elucidation of the interplay and relationship between being and non-being assumes a fundamental importance in terms of a negative ontology and a negative theology.

As already shown, the fourfold division of nature expressed through the movement of exitus and reditus provides the basic framework for a broad explanation of Eriugena's ideas. However, one further framework outlined at the beginning of the *Periphyseon* clarifies, indeed precedes, the four divisions of natura and shows clearly the double aspect of each of them: the five modes of being and non-being. The dialectical tension between being and non-being is one of the great innovative themes of the *Periphyseon*, and indeed it can be regarded as the primary framework against which Eriugena's metaphysical scheme can be examined. It is because of the constant tension between the concepts of being and non-being, in the sense that non-being becomes being while remaining non-being, that we can conclude that Eriugena's understanding of these concepts is more differentiated than that of other authors before him; indeed it is not until the fourteenth century that a similar account of the relationship between being and non-being appears in Meister Eckhart's thought.[13] Eriugena's understanding of the divine essence, the ultimate ground of reality, as *nihil*, or non-being, which itself lies beyond being and non-being, will guide him in developing a negative ontology, which was profoundly influenced by his reading of Gregory of Nyssa.[14]

In the *Periphyseon* we find that Eriugena rejects the interpretation of non-being in the privative sense (an interpretation that will be familiar to readers of Augustine on evil and a theme discussed by Eriugena in the treatise *On Predestination*).[15] There is no doubt that Eriugena was strongly influenced by Greek thought in this regard, especially the Pseudo-Dionysius and Gregory of Nyssa, but it is also likely that a Western source, the treatise by Fredegisus, successor of Alcuin, *Letter on Nothing and Darkness*, where Fredegisus argues that nihil refers to something (that from which God created), would also have steered Eriugena's interpretation in the transcendent direction.[16]

The five modes of interpretation of the relationship between being and non-being, although not exhaustive, apply to all of natura: that which can be said to be and that which can be said not to be. The first mode asserts that all things that can be sensed or understood are said to be, but those things that, because of the excellence of their nature, elude both sense and intellect, can be said not to be (P. I 443A–D). "Not to be" refers not to what is absolutely not in the privative sense—"for how can that which absolutely is not, and cannot be . . . be included in the division of things?"—but refers to it in the transcendent sense and refers to God (and matter) and the reasons or essences of all things created by God.[17] The illustrations used to clarify this important point are taken from the Pseudo-Dionysius and Gregory of Nyssa: God, the being above being, is the essence of all things, and no essence can be understood as to what it is.[18] Here Eriugena stresses the idea that what can be sensed or understood is really an "accident" added to an essence that makes it known *that* the essence is, not *what* it is, a theme I discuss hereafter. This first mode of being and non-being has important consequences for many of the ideas outlined in the *Periphyseon* and is not simply a reformulation of the Dionysian understanding of God's being as non-being in the transcendent sense. Because the divine essence is unknowable to the human mind, it can be truly said not to be. The following four modes of being and non-being are based on the first and can be understood as different elaborations of it.

The second mode, which relates to created natures, assumes a vertical hierarchy in reality and is based on the general Neoplatonic principle that the negation of a lower order involves the affirmation of a higher order; the affirmation of a lower order is the negation of a higher order; the affirmation of a higher order is the negation of a lower order; and the negation of a higher order is the affirmation of a lower order (P. I 444A–C). Eriugena illustrates this point by noting that the affirmation of "man," as a rational mortal animal, means that an angel is not a rational, mortal animal. What "man" is, angel is not, and what angel is, "man" is not. The same rule can be applied to all the orders of natura within two limits. On proceeding downward, the last order confirms or denies the order above it since there is nothing below it; on proceeding upward one reaches a halt at the highest negation,"for its negation confirms the existence of no higher creature."[19] According to Eriugena, the negation of the first of the three orders of angels (there are three orders and three groups of angels in each order) ends in pure negation since it cannot affirm a higher order. A second aspect of the second mode assumes a fundamental importance in terms of the unknowability of God. Every rational or intellectual order can be said to be in so far as it is known by the orders above it and by itself, but can be said not to be as it does not permit itself to be known by the orders below it. This idea of the hierarchy of being and non-being, therefore, does not depend on a strict Neoplatonic progression whereby each order is somehow contained in the order above it but rather has a more precise focus on the definitions of things. The example Eriugena gives makes this point clearly: what a human being is, an angel is not. In similar fashion, we can say that what God is, a human being is not and thereby affirm God's being and the non-being of human beings. Eriugena will later argue that only God truly is, while created nature exists through participation in God (P. III 646B). This mode of being and non-being, when regarded from the perspective of negative theology, adds a further dimension to the understanding of non-being. When human being is affirmed, God is understood to be non-being, and when God's "being" is affirmed, human beings can be understood as non-being. Thus, both senses of non-being operate on the same level within this particular mode.

The third mode of being and non-being refers to visible realities in existence and potential realities that still exist in their causes (P. I 444D–445A). Created effects in generation can be said to be, while that which is not yet manifest in matter, form, time, and place (that which is still held in the "most secret folds of nature") can be said not to be. The example Eriugena uses to explain this point is the original creation of human beings. In creating Adam, God established all human beings at the same time, yet not all were brought into being at the same time. From the general nature (Adam), human beings are brought into visible essences at certain predetermined times and places. Thus, those who are visibly manifest in the world are said to be, while those who are destined to be in the future can be said not to be. The important difference, as Eriugena himself notes, between the first and third modes is that the first refers to all things once and for all made in their causes, while the third refers to those that are partly hidden in their causes and partly manifest. A further example is taken from the physical world. Seeds that are not yet manifest as that which they will become can be said not to be; when they have become a tree or plant, they can be said to be.

The fourth mode, in true Platonic fashion, asserts that only those things that can be contemplated by the intellect can be said to be, while those things that are in generation, that come into being and pass away, are said not to be truly (P. I 445B–445C). An important consequence of this mode of being and non-being is that all things can be said to be since they are known by the divine intellect, an important point, which I discuss in chapter 4.

The fifth mode concerns human nature itself, which, through the fall from paradise, lost its divine image, its true being, and can, therefore, be said not to be. When human nature is restored through the grace of God, it is reestablished in its image and begins to be. This mode also refers to those whom God calls daily to be from the secret folds of nature.

The interpretation of these modes and their place in the overall scheme of the *Periphyseon* is perplexing. Eriugena appears to be setting the scene for future discussion in that many of the fundamental themes of the *Periphyseon* are derived from these basic principles, but the modes themselves are not explicitly invoked in relation to the further development of certain themes. However, the first mode assumes the greatest importance in terms of the understanding of divine reality as non-being in the transcendent sense. One further important point is that through the elucidation of these five modes Eriugena clearly shows that being and non-being, while contradictory, are in a sense resolved, not only in God who is above both being and non-being and at the same time is being and non-being, but also at every level of reality, depending on one's starting point. Eriugena's exposition of these modes can be regarded as a perspectival approach, as Dermot Moran notes: "sometimes being comes out as greater than non-being, and sometimes it is the other way round."[20] The lengthy discussion of nihil in book III of the *Periphyseon*, which I treat in chapter 4 in relation to the creative activity of God, elaborates Eriugena's basic understanding of non-being as the transcendent being of God from which God created all things. While we could argue that Eriugena's interpretation of the concepts of being and non-being is, as Moran suggests, "deeply subversive of the metaphysical tenet of the primacy of being," a reading of Eriugena in his historical context would question this conclusion.[21] Given the fact that the "primacy of being" would really only be established in the Western tradition by Aquinas in the thirteenth century, and that the Greek fathers (and some Western thinkers) had already engaged in a form of speculation that stressed the importance of non-being in the transcendent sense, it would be misleading to suggest that Eriugena was consciously attempting to formulate an alternative metaphysics. However, when Eriugena's speculations on the dialectical interplay between being and non-being are viewed in terms of the later development of philosophy, it is certain that his contribution to this particular theme, although unfortunately neglected for the most part, was innovative and can be read as an alternative to a metaphysics based on Exodus 3:14.

Negative Ontology

It is clear that Eriugena gives a privileged place to non-being in terms of an understanding of all reality. In fact, while it can be argued, as Moran does, that Eriugena constructs a radical meontology, it can also be said that he constructs a more "open" metaphysical system in line with the authorities of the Greek tradition. Otten, on the other hand, does not believe that Eriugena's use of non-being can be said to constitute a negative ontology; her view is that non-being reflects a problem of language.[22] However, given Eriugena's views on the unknowability of all *ousia*, I believe that we can describe his ontology as negative. How? Eriugena's negative understanding of ousia (essence) was inspired by Gregory of Nyssa, who developed the notion that ousia is unknowable in response to the Eunomian belief that the father's ousia could be known through the appellation "ungenerate." For Gregory, no ousia could be known in any sense. Eriugena's approach to all realities that can be understood within the overall concept of natura begins with a systematic examination of the constitution of things: a precise examination of the ten categories.[23] The discussion of negative and positive theology in *Periphyseon* book I concludes with the statement that God's essence, God's "whatness," cannot be defined. This leads directly to a discussion of the categories where Eriugena notes at the outset, following Augustine, that these cannot be applied to God (P. I 463B–C). If any of the categories were applied to God, God could be understood to be a genus. In the same way that God is understood to be more than being, God is also understood to be more than each of the categories, although categories are often attributed to God by analogy precisely because God is cause. Therefore, while Eriugena is clear that the categories cannot be attributed to God according to the rules of negative theology, the fact that they are often applied metaphorically is consequent upon God's causal activity; they provide, as John Marenbon notes, "a sourcebook of cataphatic theology."[24]

According to Eriugena's understanding, what the human mind can know about things stems from the fact that they are differentiated and can be defined: they possess quality, quantity, and relations, are limited, are in place and time, and so on. In other words, we can define things according to the circumstances or accidents that differentiate them one from the other (P. I 471C). Relying on Gregory of Nyssa, Eriugena explains that "matter is nothing else but a certain composition of accidents which proceeds from invisible causes to visible matter" (P. I 479B). Form is the measurement imposed on unformed matter that places it within the realm of limitation and definition: "whether one call it place or limit or term or definition or circumscription, one and the same thing is denoted, namely the confine of a finite creature" (P. I 483C). "Whatness," then, is concerned with limitation and pertains only to finite realities that are limited by "where?" and "when?" (P. I 482C). "There is no creature, whether visible or invisible, which is not confined in something within the limits of its proper nature by measure and number and weight" (P. II 590A–B). It is precisely the limitation of finitude that enables definition to take place. Because God is infinite, it follows that God cannot be defined. "But God understands that He is in none of those things but recognises that He [is] above all the orders of nature by reason of the excellence of His wisdom, and below all things by reason of the depth of His power. . . . He alone is the measure without measure, the number without number, and the weight without weight" (P. II 590B).

Ousia, the most important of the categories as treated by Eriugena, is incorporeal in itself, just as are all the categories when considered in themselves; it is only when some of them come together (quantity, quality, situation, and condition) that they become accessible to the bodily senses (P. I 479A).[25] Ousia is indefinable, but the things associated with it enable one to say that something is, not what it is (P. I 487A–B). Thus, the logic of negative theology becomes clear: God, as the essence of all, is known only from created things, but this is knowledge not of what God is but simply that God is. Given the primary understanding that the ousia of any thing is unknowable, it stands to reason that the essence of all things is unknowable since that very essence is God. Indeed, the substance of all things is the reason by which they subsist in the primordial causes in the Word (P. IV 772B). This idea will assume greater significance in terms of human nature's understanding of itself: as I show in chapter 6, the incomprehensibility of ousia extends also to the ousia of human being (P. IV 772B).

Eriugena's negative ontology provides the framework for an understanding of all that can be said of God's self-creative process. While it is certain that he took much from Gregory of Nyssa and the Pseudo-Dionysius, Eriugena's own unique perspective can be seen in his continual straining toward that which is truly no thing. All that can be said of the creative manifestation of God must be regulated by the understanding that while God is the essence of all things, God's ousia remains above all things in transcendent unknowability. The tension that is set up between the unknowability of ousia and theophany, as the appearance of the God who is the essence of all things, will become an important principle in relation to a correct interpretation of created reality. The importance of understanding the very building blocks of reality in terms of being and non-being is that it does not present the reader with a static concept or one final way of interpreting reality. Just when we think that we have understood something, Eriugena loosens our grip on what has been understood by introducing another perspective, and what has been grasped slips away into the unbounded territory of negative theology where all concepts are fluid and nothing is final. If we read the *Periphyseon* with the basic principles of negative theology in mind, then we will not stray far from a correct interpretation of some of the more difficult concepts examined by the nutritor and his inquisitive yet extremely astute alumnus.

4

CREATOR AND CREATION

I have shown that Eriugena's conception of the divine nature is characterized by the dual truth of the simultaneous immanence and transcendence
of God, a theme he encountered more strongly in the writings of the Greek
than in the Latin fathers. Of course, Eriugena's thought was not simply a re-
production of what he had encountered in his reading of the fathers of East
and West; rather, he molded their theology into his own to reveal a new pat-
tern of thought in relation to an understanding of the transcendence and
immanence of God. The four divisions of nature, the first and last of which
contemplate God under the aspects of first cause and final end, necessarily
relate to God in terms of created reality: either the coming forth from God or
the returning to God. The fourfold division of nature, which provides the
fundamental structure of the *Periphyseon,* is understood from the starting
point of God's creative activity, the manifestation of uncreated natura, and
all theological speculation must be understood in relation to the process of
creation.

The Uncreated Creator

The uncreated creator, the first cause of all causes, is unknowable, unnameable, and ineffable. The term "uncreated" points the way to a proper dialectical understanding of divine reality: God can be known as creator but remains
unknowable as uncreated, even to God's self, a theme I discuss hereafter. Thus,
nothing at all can be thought or said of the uncreated aspect of God's nature,
except, as I will show, statements that do not affirm anything of God in a
limited, definitional sense. All theology, therefore, must take as its starting point
the manifestation of God in theophany. For Eriugena, the term "God" refers

both to the divine essence unknowable in itself (God's ousia), and to the mode in which God reveals God's self (the theophany or apparition of God) in created effects (P. I 446C–D). Therefore, we can know of and speak about God's creative activity; it is precisely this aspect of Eriugena's thought that is most fascinating and challenging, especially for contemporary readers more familiar with later scholastic medieval thought. According to Eriugena, even though God's nature is unknowable, God can in a very real sense be known through God's effects, although that truth is subject to repeated denial throughout the *Periphyseon:* God is equally incomprehensible "when considered in the innermost depths of the creature which was made by Him and which exists in Him" (P. I 443B). Therefore, the reality of the divine nature is that it cannot be understood in itself, and it both can and cannot be understood when contemplated in created effects. From this standpoint I begin my examination of the creation process of the uncreated as outlined in the *Periphyseon*, remembering that "where it is beyond our reach and does not suffer itself to be observed and elucidated by minds that are still weighed down by their earthly habitation it should be respected in the silence of our hearts and our lips lest we should give some rational explanation of it" (P. III 638D).

Creation *ex Nihilo* and Theophany

> And therefore even that matter from which it is read that He made the world is from Him and in Him, and He is in it in so far as it is understood to have being. (P. II 579A)

The theme of creation is central to an understanding of Eriugena's thought, indeed it is the starting point of the great metaphysical epic that is the *Periphyseon*. Eriugena's understanding of the creative activity of God, as elaborated especially in *Periphyseon* book III, is refreshingly relevant, even at the dawn of a new millennium. In fact, it could be said that Eriugena's understanding of divine (and human) reality, when viewed in the light of contemporary thought, opens up a new perspective on the typically neoscholastic perception of medieval thought.[1] According to Eriugena, creation is the fundamental starting point for any attempt to understand divine reality (Rom. 1:20), and it constitutes the one great mystery that focuses his thought as he attempts to set down, in an orderly fashion, sure definitions and right knowledge of the things that are. The act of creation by God, the cause of causes, is creation *ex nihilo:* God creates all things out of the "superessential nothingness" that God transcendently is. This idea, which Eriugena would have encountered especially in the works of the Pseudo-Dionysius and Gregory of Nyssa, is elaborated in the fascinating treatise on nothing in *Periphyseon* book III and is extremely important for an understanding of his concept of God's creative activity. The conclusions Eriugena draws from this fundamental thesis form an important preamble to the discussion of creation itself but, more important, lead to his ultimate conclusion that God is all things.

"Nothing," in a typically apophatic understanding, is the divine essence, not by privation, but in the excellent sense. However, although we can say that God is nothing, paradoxically, God is more than being (P. III 634B). "I should believe that by that name is signified the ineffable and incomprehensible and inaccessible brilliance of the Divine Goodness . . . which while it is contemplated in itself neither is nor was nor shall be, for it is understood to be in none of the things that exist because it surpasses all things . . . " (P. III 680D–681A). This understanding of nothing, the superlative, transcendent, ineffable, incomprehensible, and inaccessible brilliance of the divine goodness (P. III 680D), is derived principally from the Pseudo-Dionysius and is later developed more fully by Meister Eckhart. Accordingly, "to be grasped by the mind, has become the very premise of being, while to transcend the mind's grasp serves as the premise of non-being."[2] The insistence on a superlative rather than privative understanding of nothingness in relation to God reveals a basic tension in terms of describing the divine essence as nothing (for it is literally no-thing) and as cause: everything has a cause and must come from something rather than nothing (P. III 664A). Eriugena explains that according to traditional accounts, the nature of nothing is understood to be the negation and absence of all essence and substance (P. III 635A). However, such an understanding is not accepted by all exegetes, and rightly so, according to Eriugena, for it creates a worrying problem in relation to the idea that all things are eternal in the creativity of the divine wisdom (P. III 635A). The central problem for Eriugena here is to determine how that which begins to be in time can be in eternity (P. III 636A). Eriugena's ultimate conclusion to and resolution of this problem is that all things are at the same time eternal and are made in the Word: eternal things are made and made things are eternal (P. III 646C). The cause of the universe, the Word, both makes all things and is made in all things (P. III 646C). The alumnus is, of course, shocked by this seemingly heretical statement and rightly asks for clarification, which the nutritor gives willingly with an illustration drawn from mathematics. All numbers are said to be in the monad (the number one), both causally and eternally. Numbers can be understood, therefore, as both eternal and made: they are eternal in the monad and they are made in multiplicity (P. III 659A). Likewise, in the process of God's creative activity, the eternal begins to be in time, indeed begins to be because in itself it is no thing. Thus, the invisible becomes visible through creation (P. III 678C). As Donald Duclow puts it, "creation *ex nihilo* is therefore nothing other than creation *ex deo*; it is the manifestation, the procession of transcendent negativity into the differentiated otherness of being and essence."[3] This understanding of the ineffable descent of the supreme Goodness can, as the alumnus points out, constitute a real problem for many, even if it has the authority of the scriptures, the fathers, and right reason to support it. Is the authority of Basil of Caeserea weighty enough to support the thesis that the Word is the nature of all things and allay the reservations of those who fear to contradict orthodoxy? (P. III 685B–C). Eriugena believed, perhaps rashly, as later condemnations of the *Periphyseon* would demonstrate, that the authority of this venerable father could do precisely that.

The nothing from which all things came, when contemplated in itself, neither is nor was nor shall be because it is none of the things which exist; it simply surpasses them all (P. III 680D–681B). But when, through the creative process, it is seen in theophany, it alone is found to be in all things (P. III 681A). This is the central dialectic permeating Eriugena's conception of divine reality and creation *ex nihilo:* nothing, ineffably and incredibly, becomes not only some thing, but all things. "God is the Maker of all things and is made in all things; and when He is looked for above all things He is found in no essence—for as yet there is no essence—but when He is understood in all things nothing in them subsists but Himself alone; and 'neither is He this', as he says, 'but not that', but He is all" (P. III 683A). Here Eriugena is quoting a key passage from the *Divine Names* of the Pseudo-Dionysius in which the meaning of the self-creation of God in created effects is clarified. In this text, as Michael Sells puts it, Eriugena's own nutritor is Dionysius, and Eriugena generates an apophatic tension through "weaving key Dionysian passages into his own language."[4] Because creation is from the superessential nothingness of the divine nature, it cannot be contrary to God (the cause of all contraries), even though we must deny the truth of this affirmation in an apophatic moment by affirming that creation is other than God since God became other than God in creating. The relationship between cause and effect in Eriugena's thought can be described as a relationship of cognition between God, unknowable even to God's self (a theme I discuss hereafter), and God knowable to God's self and to other intellects and minds.

The unity of God and creature is a strong theme in the *Periphyseon,* although the division of nature itself serves to maintain a distinction between the two and is confirmation of the fact that God and creature do not exist on the same ontological level. Creation is not something apart from God, but is, as I will show, the ontological participation of the creature in God. In this sense we can say that creation is already God, already deified because its very identity is God. The distinction between the two, the difference in nature, is primarily due to the fall of human nature from its original status.[5] According to John Meyendorff, the created world is "ontologically external to God" because for Eriugena, as for the Greek fathers, "it is rooted in his [God's] will which is different from his nature."[6] As Eriugena says, "all are once and for all co-eternal save for the status of creator and created" (P. II 559B). The truth of this statement rests on the idea that while God, as cause, is "made" in God's effects, God remains above created effects in the darkness and unknowability of God's hidden essence, like the mighty Plotinian One who remains above all duality in majestic rest (*Enn.* VI 7, 39, 21).

Theophany, as the manifestation of the hidden and the becoming visible of the invisible, is the "ineffable descent of the Supreme Goodness, which is Unity and Trinity, into the things that are so as to make them to be, indeed so as itself to be" (P. III 678D). Theophany, the appearance of God (P. I 446C–D), becomes the means whereby knowledge of and speech about God are possible, and the discussion of theophany that occurs so early in book I of the *Periphyseon* is an indication of the fact that it is central to a correct understanding of Eriugena's interpretation of created and uncreated reality. The nutritor prefaces his account of theophany by stating that he knows of no "deeper thing there can be for human inquiry" (P. I 449A). The divine nature, which is invisible and incomprehensible in itself, becomes visible and comprehensible when it creates itself as other in an other. Eriugena explains this difficult point using an analogy derived from Maximus the Confessor. Just as air that is illuminated by the sun is invisible because it appears to be light, so too when the divine essence (invisible in itself) is joined to an intellectual creature it alone is seen (P. I 450A and *Hom.* XIII 290C–D).[7] All things that can be understood are God's manifestation of God's hidden nature, expressed by Eriugena in some of the most dialectical passages in the *Periphyseon*:

> For everything that is understood and sensed is nothing else but the apparition of what is not apparent, the manifestation of the hidden, the affirmation of the negated, the comprehension of the incomprehensible, [the utterance of the unutterable, the access to the inaccessible,] the understanding of the unintelligible, the body of the bodiless, the essence of the superessential, the form of the formless, the measure of the measureless, the number of the unnumbered, the weight of the weightless, the materialization of the spiritual, the visibility of the invisible. (P. III 633A, 678C)

Used as we are to understanding the divine nature from either one perspective or the other, these Eriugenian formulations (though by no means original to him), stretch the mind in both directions simultaneously, for the one cannot be understood without the other: God both is all things and is not all things.[8] The idea that God is manifest in creation is true, and the fact that God remains transcendently unmanifest is also true. And yet, neither are true when understood singly; the "problem" is resolved by coupling both truths in a dialectical formulation that reveals the tension between, and the simultaneous truth, of both. The "path" Eriugena takes to God via theophany is, therefore, a path that is filled with signs and symbols of the presence of the unmanifest God made manifest. To understand this gives one a clearer conception of the far-reaching conclusions of Eriugena's thought in relation to the creative activity of the uncreated. The truth of the statement "God is all things" is constantly undermined by the basic distinction between the divine essence and theophany, which is a forceful reminder that as an apophatic understanding demonstrates, a comprehensive account of reality can never be attained. All that is said about the creative process in the *Periphyseon* is constantly under threat from the continuous moments of denial that something can be said about the divine nature. The noetic tension between the simultaneous knowability and unknowability of God is a constant feature of Eriugena's thought that cannot be explained away, indeed cannot be explained further as it is grounded in an ontological conception of how "nothing" creates all otherness and difference. Eriugena's Neoplatonism is strongly evident with respect to this dialectical understanding of divine reality. However, the continual assertion that God is all things is placed firmly in a Christian perspective as Eriugena explains how the triune nature of God effects the creative process.

Trinitarian Causality in the Word

"[A]ll things are from Him and through Him and in Him and for Him." (P. III 679A)

According to Eriugena, the beginning of all creative activity is trinitarian, that is, God makes all things coeternally in the Word (P. II 556B; IV 786B). The frequent discussions of the nature of the Trinity in the *Periphyseon* are not an unnecessary theological digression but are essential for a correct understanding of the creative process that Eriugena bases firmly in the scriptures, and Eriugena uses five seminal scriptural texts to help explain the creative process in the *Periphyseon*.[9] "In the beginning was the Word, and the Word was with God, and the Word was God. He was in the beginning with God. All things came into being through Him, and without Him not one thing came into being. What has come into being in Him was life" (John 1:1–4). "[F]or in Him all things in heaven and on earth were created, things visible and invisible" (Col. 1:16). "O Lord, how manifold are your works! In wisdom you have made them all" (Ps. 104:24). "In the beginning when God created the heavens and the earth" (Gen. 1:1).[10] "In the beginning, in the day of your power, in sacred splendours before the daystar in the womb I begot you" (Ps. 110:3).[11] In his explanation of these texts as the basis for his interpretation of the six first days of creation we see Eriugena's originality in terms of scriptural exegesis at its very best and most enterprising.

The hexaemeral commentary begun in book III and completed in book IV, although long awaited—it was promised in book II (556A) and delayed until III (690C)—is full of surprises even for the exegete of today. Although Eriugena relies heavily on the patristic sources of both East and West (Basil of Caeserea, Gregory of Nyssa, and Augustine feature most in Eriugena's reviews of previous exegeses of the text of Genesis 1), Eriugena's own ideas are clearly seen in relation to the mysterious nature of the creative activity of the triune divine nature. According to John J. O'Meara, "Eriugena and Augustine are fundamentally at one in their approach to the problem of creation: both start out from apophaticism"; the fundamental difference between the two is that Augustine's approach is historical and Eriugena's theoretical.[12] The commentary on the six first days also demonstrates Eriugena's erudition and knowledge of natural science: the nature of the celestial bodies, the measurement of the planets, and cosmic distances (he relies chiefly, though not exclusively, on Pliny and Martianus Capella). In the lengthy digression on measurement and cosmic distances, perhaps of more interest to the historian of the philosophy of science, which eventually tires the nutritor, who must be prompted to continue by the alumnus (P. III 715B–726A), natural science also comes under the scrutiny (albeit fleetingly) of negative theology (P. III 723B). Eriugena feels it necessary to point out that even though an apophatic attitude is at the heart of Ecclesiasticus 1:3 (who has measured God's handiwork?), in this instance, the primacy of an apophatic moment does not prevail. Other scriptural texts are invoked as an apology for undertaking the enterprise of cosmic measurement, primarily Romans 1:20. The spoils of the Egyptians (natural science) can, therefore, be used to good effect in the search for truth (P. III 724A)—an interpretation Eriugena encountered in Augustine's *On Christian Doctrine* (II 40, 60–61). In addition, the two vestments of Christ at the transfiguration (Matt. 17:2), can be interpreted as the letter of the scriptures and physical reality: we can, therefore, investigate one to find out about the other.

Eriugena's interpretation of Psalm 110:3 (in the beginning, in the womb I begot you) is, to my mind, the most important text for a correct understanding of divine generation: "With Thee and in Thee is eternally the Beginning of all (things), that is, Thy Word" (P. II 557A; IV 834B). Irrespective of the discrepancies between the Hebrew, Septuagint, and Latin versions of this particular text, no doubt Eriugena was drawn to it because it allowed him to forge a further link between the generation of all things in the beginning with the mysterious generation of the ineffable Word from the father's womb. It also provides the occasion for a comment on the link between the primordial daystar (understood by Eriugena to signify the whole physical world) mentioned in the psalm and the star visible at the birth of the Word (P. II 559C–560A). According to Eriugena's interpretation, the father begets the son eternally from the secret recesses of his womb, his substance (P. II 558A–B) (an interesting use of female imagery that does not occasion further comment) and simultaneously creates the causes of all things in the Word (P. II 561C). This particular text focuses on an extremely apt way to describe that mysterious generation that takes place in secret and in darkness and which no one (at least no one in the ninth century) could see or comprehend. The generation of the Word, then, is an incomprehensible process known only to the begetter and the begotten: "For no man nor any of the celestial powers, can know of the generation of the Word from the Father" (P. II 557C). In the Word were simultaneously created the primordial causes, the reasons for all things created. The spirit, the proceeding, is the distributor of the causes (P. II 563C–D; III 672C–D) and ensures that all are allocated in proportion—I will show later how the return of all things also takes place according to proportion (and capacity).

The father, the unbegotten and begetting, the son, the begotten, and the spirit, the proceeding, reflect in dialectical fashion the method of the division of nature in the *Periphyseon* (P. I 456B–C, 490A–B; II 600A). The father is "the cause of causes": the cause of the cause that is born and the cause of the cause that proceeds (P. II 600B). It is in relation to his explanation of divine generation as a prelude to the discussion of the generation of all things that we find Eriugena broaching the subject of the filioque problem that had caused so much dissension the previous century (P. II 601B–615C). In view of his general liking for and attraction to Greek ideas, Eriugena concludes, despite his reluctance to show his hand too clearly in relation to this most difficult of topics, that the spirit proceeds from the father through the son (from one cause): *ex patre per filium.*[13] Part of his argument rests on the nature of causality in the physical world, where things cannot have two causes (P. II 608C–609A). In response to the relentless probing questions of the alumnus, the nutritor argues that the spirit proceeds from the substance of the father, not from the father's essence. Here it is clear that Eriugena's discussion of ousia and *hypostasis* rests on the acceptance of the Greek formulation of Trinity: one ousia and three substances (P. I 456B). However, lest we think that the discussion of the nature of the Trinity has been concluded, Eriugena is quick to point out that any attempt to resolve the differences between the Latin and Greek formulas simply points up the essential mystery of trinitarian generation. In addition to examining the nature of internal procession within the Trinity, Eriugena also brings up the subject of a much older problem concerning the names of the Trinity, the last vestige of a very old debate between Eunomius and the Cappadocian fathers. He concludes, not surprisingly, in agreement with Gregory of Nyssa, that the names "father," "son," and "spirit" do not signify natures or operations but are relational (P. I 456C–457D; IV 794C–D). In this "clearing of the decks" for further discussion, Eriugena's Greek sympathies can be clearly discerned, a characteristic that can be detected time and time again in the *Periphyseon* though not without the obvious evidence of some discomfort as he is often forced to explain the differences between the fathers of East and West.

The triune nature of divine causality is reflected in the repeated assertion that the father is, the son is wise (in "wisdom" God made all things), and the spirit lives (P. I 455C); another important formulation used by Eriugena is that the father wills, the son makes, and the spirit perfects (P. II 553C–D). "So before this visible world proceeded through generation into the genera and species and all the sensible individuals, God the Father before the secular ages (began), brought forth His Word, in Whom and through Whom He created in their full perfection the primordial causes of all natures" (P. II 560A–B). The Word, therefore, is the principle through whom the father "speaks" the creation of all things (P. III 642B) and is the first principle of divisoria running through all things that they may be (P. III 642D), just as the Word is also the first principle of resolutiva (P. II 526B–C). In this sense, the logical method of dialectic—division and resolution—is prefigured in the activity of the Word itself. However, Eriugena is very clear that the causal activity of the Trinity does not imply that the Trinity is one and one and one; rather, it is a simple and indivisible one, multiple in power, not in number (P. III 687C–D). Eriugena does not wish to deny three in order to reach one as the Pseudo-Dionysius had done. Thus, the trinitarian concept of causality in the *Periphyseon,* which is most Dionysian in inspiration, as the cosmic force that gives life to the world, is also the source of the tension between causality and transcendence. In the specifically Christian sense, the philosophical problem of how unity gives rise to multiplicity can be found in the doctrine of the Trinity. The three in one, the inner structure of the unity itself, explains the whole process of causality.[14] For Eriugena then, Trinity explains not only the process of cosmic salvation and return through the *inhumanatio* of the Word but also, and perhaps primarily, the process of creation itself as an operation of the triune God.

The Primordial Causes and Participation

The primordial causes in Eriugena's thought are Platonic in character, like Augustine's *rationes aeternae,* and can be understood as the ideas or predestinations of all things in the mind of God made in the Word.[15] "So the principal causes of all things are co-eternal with God and with the Beginning in which they were made. For if God does not in any way precede the Beginning, that is the Word begotten by Himself and from Himself, and the Word does not in any way precede the causes of things that are created in it, it follows that all these . . . are co-eternal" (P. II 561B–C). The primordial causes are the species or forms in which the reasons are created before the things themselves existed (P. II 529B). Toward the end of book II of the *Periphyseon* (616C) and again early in book III (622B–623C), Eriugena lists the primordial causes, showing once again his indebtedness to the Pseudo-Dionysius.[16] Their order, he notes, is simply a mental arrangement so that we can say something about them, although the first three remain the most important and are ordered as follows: Goodness-through-itself, Being-through-itself, and Life-through-itself. After these come Reason, Intellect, Wisdom, Power, Blessedness, Justice, Truth,

Eternity, Magnitude, Peace, Love, Omnipotence, Unity, Perfection, and all the powers and reasons made by the father in the Word. Eriugena illustrates the unity between the causes and between the causes and their effects through the image of a circle, used also by the Pseudo-Dionysius.[17] The image of a circle with radii from the center, as in an old-fashioned cartwheel, illustrates the diversity of created effects, which are simultaneously held together in the Word at their meeting point in the hub of the wheel. The causes, therefore, both remain in the Word and move outward into created effects. Eriugena also uses this illustration to explain how the primordial causes are both same and different. In themselves, the primordial causes are one and simple (in the center of the circle), and no one knows their order save their creator (P. II 624C–D, 626C).

In book III of the *Periphyseon*, Eriugena raises the very interesting question of whether the primordial causes were made of nothing in the Word or were always in the Word, a question which itself raises a number of perplexing points for discussion. Eriugena is clear in his refutation of the heretical idea that "nothing" existed coeternally with God (P. III 664C) because God *is* the nothing from which all things were made. The causes were always as causes in the Word potentially, and at the same time they were not always because they flowed through generation into forms, species, places, and time. Therefore, they always were, and they began to be (P. III 665B–C). They can be said to be coeternal with God since they always subsist in God; they have no beginning in time, and yet they are not coeternal with God because they receive their beginning from the uncreated creator in the Word. Therefore, they can be understood as simultaneous with but not coessential with God (P. II 561D–562A). The father precedes the origins of the things made in the Word, and the Word precedes the things made because the maker always precedes the made (P. II 562B).

In his discussion of the role of the primordial causes, Eriugena begins with Genesis 1:1 (P. II 546A–548A). In the beginning, that is, in the Word, the causes of the whole creature were made perfectly and immutable, ever turned toward the Word of the father. The idea that the causes are eternally formed in the Word and always contemplate the Word, which is above them, means that they are held in being eternally by the Word (P. II 547C). In similar fashion, the things that the primordial causes create are constantly drawn up toward them in order to seek the cause. This natural compulsion is inherent in the very structure of all created effects.

In the Genesis text concerning the first day of creation, as examined in *Periphyseon* books II and III, Eriugena interprets the original "waste and void over the abyss" as signifying the perfection of the primordial nature created before all things in the Word (P. II 549B). Since the primordial causes were created in the beginning (in the Word) by the cause of causes, they themselves, in their eternal aspect, are still a "dark abyss," covered with a cloud of darkness because of the ineffable excellence of their purity and their infinite mysterious diffusion through all things.[18] As the causes of all things manifest in the brightness of the appearance of God, they still remain dark because they cannot be perceived by any other intellect except their cause. Their effects show that they are but not what they are (P. II 551A). Therefore, the primordial causes are both knowable and unknowable, hidden by the excessive brightness of the divine wisdom (P. III 623D; 1 Tim. 6:16) and yet "seen" in their effects. The *fiat lux* of Genesis 1:3 heralds their procession into created effects as they effect the movement from darkness to light, from invisibility to visibility, from unknowability to knowability (P. III 692A–693C). In dividing light from darkness, God separated the knowledge of effects from the obscurity of their causes, which are hidden and united in the Word. This concept can be understood to imply the sanctification of all created things and is an aspect of Eriugena's thought that could be appealing today as a further source for a sound Christian environmental ethic. All creation is holy, not simply because it was created by God in the Word but because it was created from God: all things made in God are God (P. III 675B). Eriugena, like Augustine and the Pseudo-Dionysius, uses the seminal Pauline text, Romans 1:20, as the basis for the idea that the visible shows forth the invisible: "from the creation of the world His invisible things are seen, being understood from the things that have been made" (P. III 723B). "There is no visible or corporeal thing which is not the symbol of something incorporeal and intelligible" (P. V 865D–866A). All of creation has a "sacramental" value as a sign of the divine nature. In fact, Eriugena notes that Plato was led from visible realities to discover the creator (P. III 724B). As Duclow has remarked, "conceived as theophany, the entire created order becomes a field of translucent symbols which yield knowledge of the divine nature."[19]

The diffusion of the causes is effected through the activity of the spirit, who precedes the "mystical waters" (understood as the primordial causes) of Genesis. The spirit eternally ferments and fertilizes the causes in the spirit's self (P. II 536D). Eriugena's exegesis of the fermenting/fertilizing capacity of the spirit is based on the Hebrew and Septuagint versions of the Genesis text (the Latin version has "borne above"). The spirit is responsible for the diffusion of the causes into multiplicity in an eternal activity of ordering and harmonization. Thus the Trinity, unknowable to every creature, descends to become known and present to every intellect (P. II 579A–B).

Eriugena explains how the four elements of the world, having been created through the primordial causes, occupy an intermediate position between the causes and composite bodies, subsist in their causes (P. III 663D), and are distributed throughout the sensible world, an idea he found in Gregory of Nyssa. The elements are subject to divine laws, though Eriugena admits that he cannot explain precisely how. Given the fact that the generation of things in the changing seasons of the year is difficult to explain, it is not surprising that procession from God is a mystery to the human mind (P. III 669C–D). Such statements of cognitive failure in the face of mystery, which are found throughout the *Periphyseon*, are not simply a way of avoiding difficult problems but rather are very powerful indicators that mystery governs the very heart of created (and uncreated) reality. "The mystery of being, of life, and of consciousness is unfathomable. No mind, not even the mind of the deity, can fully comprehend these mysteries."[20] Eriugena's sense of fascination with and wonder about the physical world is evident in many pages of the *Periphyseon*: all things follow divine laws, which surpass sense and intellect and are mysterious to the human mind (P. III 669C). Ultimately, the establishment of all things in the Word is a mystery that the human mind can only hint at through astute reasoning about and observation of created effects (P. III 670A). How can anyone attempt to explain the "first downrush simultaneously into the initial constitution of this world" which occurred in the "blink of an eye" (P. III 699B)? What we understand in temporal terms as the six first days of creation was a single instantaneous act, not divided by intervals of time (P. III 708C; IV 848A–B).

However, despite the mysterious origins and working of the universe, reason and observation can deduce that from nothing God called all things into essence in a fivefold motion of creation through the primordial causes in the Word. Natural bodies (rocks, mountains, and other inanimate effects) are called simply to subsist; trees and plants are called to subsist and to live; irrational animals also have sense in addition to subsisting and life; in human beings, reason is added to all these, and in the angelic nature, intellect is added. It is in this fivefold creative process (interestingly, one account of the return in *Periphyseon* book V (876A–B) elaborates five stages also) that the goodness of God is seen in creation (P. II 580D). Eriugena also outlines other articulations of the creation process: the insensitive (plants), the sensitive (animals), the rational (human beings), and the intellectual (angels) (P. III 732C–733B), and a tripartite version whereby all created nature consists of the wholly spirit (reasons), the wholly body (physical realities), and the intermediate (both body and spirit) (P. II 695A–B). In whatever way Eriugena explains it, he is always conscious to show that the whole of created reality is harmoniously knit together in the secret and ineffable unity of the Word.

According to the picture emerging from Eriugena's exposition, one can see the hierarchy of the world order he envisaged, an order that reflects his general reliance on the Pseudo-Dionysius: the Word, the primordial causes, angelic intellects, and human nature. The whole of creation is ordered from the highest to the lowest (P. III 683B); as it progresses "downward," the divine nature becomes more visible as God is made in God's effects. And yet a hierarchial intelligible order is not an accurate account of how Eriugena envisages the creative process of the triune God. To employ the analogy of the circle once more, we could say that the point, which can be so small as to be invisible to the naked eye, and which slowly spirals upwards in an ever-increasing circular movement, is closer to the thought Eriugena is struggling to express.

In book II of the *Periphyseon*, Eriugena once again has recourse to the spatial imagery favored by many Neoplatonists to explain the diffusion of the primordial causes through the spirit (P. III 631A–632D). The descent downward has two important components: gift and grace, which Eriugena derives from his reading of the Pseudo-Dionysius based on James 1:17: "[e]very generous act of giving, with every perfect gift, is from above, coming down from the Father of Lights."[21] Gifts descend from the unbegotten light, through the begotten light and the proceeding light. According to Eriugena's interpretation, gift (*datum*) is the initial constitution of all things in being, while grace (*donum*) represents the virtues by which nature is adorned. This distinction between gift and grace assumes even greater importance in the context of the return of all things to their source. Being descends as the gift of God, as that by which every nature subsists; through the grace of God, well-being is that by which every subsisting nature is adorned. Goodness bestows not only the gift of being and the grace of well-being but also, as I will show, the gift of eternal being (P. V 903C–904A). The gift of being and the grace of well-being, which all creatures possess, means that everything participates in goodness and in grace: "in goodness that they may be, in grace that they may be both good and beautiful" (P. III 631B). Being and well-being, then, constitute the foundations of reality as they descend from the causes to the lowest order of creation. That means that they are the only causes to do so: wisdom, intellect, and reason do not.

However, creative activity does not end with the simple giving of gift or grace; created natures must be continuously sustained in being. According to Eriugena's conception, God's creative activity can be understood only in the context of participation, which he expounds in a most Dionysian fashion. Participation becomes the key to an understanding of the central theme that God is made in all things. "For He is held to be made in His creatures generally because in them He, without Whom they cannot be, is not only understood to be, but also is their essence" (P. I 516B). Participation explains how the causes relate to their created effects: what is good is good through participation in the Good-through-itself. "For it is by participation in the Supreme Good and the Supreme Goodness whose image it is, that the image is both goodness and good" (P. IV 778B). Participation means to exist in God, in grace; the participation of effects in the cause means that the cause "is nothing else but the essence of all things" (P. III 645C). "For only He truly exists by Himself, and He alone is everything which in the things that are is truly said to be" (P. I 518A). In the creative process, the end of the descent of the Word is reached with the third division of nature in which can be seen the "last trace of the Divine Nature" (P. III 689C). And yet, even in the marvelous mystery that Eriugena elaborates, that God alone is all things, it is clear, as he insisted in the opening lines of book II, that God is not a genus of the creature and the creature is not a species of God. Nonetheless, metaphorically speaking, God can be said to be the genus and the whole species and part since everything comes from God and can, therefore, be said of God (P. II 524C–D). The whole process by which the creature comes from the cause of causes through the procession of the primordial causes from the Word cannot be understood in isolation from the parallel concept of the return (P. II 529A). In the return, all things find rest in their source, while paradoxically, in the outgoing from their source, things do not leave it for they exist through participation in the nature that truly exists (P. I 454A).

All things that are are either participated in or participate in something else: the creator is the unparticipated and is participated in; the primordial causes are participated in and also participate in their cause, and the effects of the primordial causes participate in their causes (P. III 630A–C). This scheme of participation can be understood as a further articulation of the first three divisions of nature; of necessity the fourth division cannot even be participated in since all things will have returned to unity in their source. In a thoroughly Neoplatonic fashion, Eriugena explains that every order participates in the order above it and in turn is participated in by the order below it. Participation can be understood as the distribution of divine gifts and graces— the distribution of being and well-being from the highest to the lowest order in creation (P. III 631A). This distribution of gifts and graces by the spirit is the proportionality existing between the whole of created reality: "the Creator of all things has constituted between the participations of the natural orders marvelous and ineffable harmonies by which all things come together into one concord" (P. III 630D). Eriugena explains that the Greek terms *metoche* and *metousia* more clearly show that participation means "the derivation from a superior essence of the essence which follows" (P. III 632B); he explains his point once again using a Neoplatonic image. A river wells up from its source and continues to flow to its end; in the same way, the primordial causes flow down through the various orders of the universe, from the higher to the lower. Although a river does not make the return journey to its source in a complementary fashion, the primordial causes "return back again to their source through the most secret channels of nature by a hidden course" (P. III 632C). In this sense, Eriugena shows that there is a fundamental interconnectedness between the various orders of reality, an interconnectedness that today finds expression in the idea that the whole biotic (and abiotic) community is related in that all things are made from "the ashes of dead stars."

Negative Theology

Thus far, I have examined Eriugena's conception of the creative process of the divine nature as a "downward" process of the lightening of the darkness of

God's unknowable being. Indeed, much of the focus of the *Periphyseon* is on the mysterious and exciting process of the appearance of God. However, the positive account of the knowability, visibility, and appearance of God is counterbalanced by Eriugena's strong insistence on the simultaneous unknowableness of God's being, in which he follows closely the Pseudo-Dionysius. Although Eriugena would have been familiar with the principles of negative theology from his reading of Augustine and other Western authors, the Pseudo-Dionysius and Maximus the Confessor exerted stronger influence on him with respect to this most important thematic.[22] Interestingly, Eriugena does not appear to have known the most apophatic works of Gregory of Nyssa, the *Sermons on the Canticle* and the *Beatitudes* and *Life of Moses*.

I have already examined the central idea that the divine essence is both transcendent and immanent, and that while God encompasses all things, in fact, is all things, God is not encompassed. God is both within and outside all things, being and nothing, similar and different, manifest and unmanifest, known and unknown. It is precisely the tension between each of these "opposites" which necessitates, for Eriugena, the primacy of a negative theology, a subject that is examined very early in *Periphyseon* book I. Positive theology can indeed affirm the truths of God's creative activity, although not entirely, for all positive statements about God rest on the fundamental logic of God's self-manifestation in creation: God is truly made in all things and can be said to be all things. Negative theology, which denies the affirmations made about the divine nature, is more exact in its focus, more powerful, and closer to the truth. "Affirmation is less capable than negation of signifying the ineffable Essence of God, seeing that by the former one among the created attributes is transferred to the Creator, whereas by the latter the Creator is conceived in Himself beyond every creature" (P. IV 758A). Time and time again, we find Eriugena struggling relentlessly with his God concepts in order to present a correct interpretation of divine reality—one that should not stray too far into the realm of affirmative theology and one that cannot rely totally on negative theology. The methodology of negative theology permeates the whole of Eriugena's thought: whatever is said about God can be contradicted, and even the contradiction can be contradicted. God is nothing; God is something; God is not nothing; God is not something.

Although in the *Periphyseon* Eriugena is concerned primarily with the manifestation of God, the mysterious, unknowable, hidden, transcendent nature of the divine essence is always evident. According to the Neoplatonic principle outlined by Eriugena early in book I, every order of nature can be said to be in so far as it is known by the orders above it and can be said not to be since it is not known by the orders below it. The human mind, therefore, cannot know the divine essence because that which knows must be greater than the known, a direct contradiction of the Augustinian principle that in relation to the existence of God, the known is greater than the knower.[23] That which has the capacity of defining something, of placing something within the realm of limit, "whatness," and finitude, must be ontologically superior. The seraphim of Isaiah 6:2 veil their faces and their feet with their wings before that which they are not permitted to know (P. III 668A–C, 614D–615A). Thus, the divine essence remains unknowable because it is not limited; it has no attributes to "clothe" it and make it a known "what." However, creation itself can be regarded as the "attribute" of God in that it makes the invisible visible, although it simply makes known that God is not what God is.

Thus, God is knowable and nameable in God's effects and unknowable and unnameable in God's essence (a very Eastern concept);[24] indeed as I have shown, according to Eriugena all ousia, not only divine ousia, is unknowable. "Nothing is more hidden than it, nothing more present, difficult as to where it is, more difficult as to where it is not, an ineffable light ever present to the intellectual eyes of all and known to no intellect as to what it is, diffused through all things to infinity, is made both all things and in all things and nothing in nothing" (P. III 681B–C). This text, reminiscent of many passages in Plotinus and Augustine, illustrates the dialectical nature of God's self. The divine descent from negation into all essences is the affirmation of the whole universe; that means that although affirmations have a certain validity, they contain a partial truth only and cannot be literally true (P. I 510C). "And if anyone who saw God understood what he saw, it would not be God that he saw but one of those creatures which derive their existence and unknowability from Him" (P. V 920C), a direct quotation from the Pseudo-Dionysius and a paraphrase of the more succinct expression: *si comprehendis, non est deus* (if you understand, it is not God). Negative statements, therefore, are more accurate when speaking about the divine nature, but do no more than affirm God's *quia est*. "[F]or there is more truth in saying that God is not any of the things that are predicated of Him than in saying that He is" (P. I 522B). Although the manifestation of God in created effects can be limited by number, weight, and measure, God's self is the number without number, the measure without measure, and the weight without weight (P. III 669B–C). Thus, Eriugena demonstrates that even given the understanding that God is all things because God made them, God cannot, as cause, be the things God has made (P. I 482A; II 589B; III 622A).

I have argued elsewhere that *apophasis* and *kataphasis* are not simply useful devices that enable human beings to speak or not speak about God but are, rather, an integral part of Eriugena's analysis of reality.[25] If God is understood as *principium*, we can speak of the outgoing from God in positive terms, but if God is taken as *finis*, negative formulations are more appropriate, while never exact. However, even when God is understood as principium, a dialectical tension is revealed in the first division of nature itself, the "uncreated creator." The human mind, as a result of its *duplex theoria* (double contemplation), considers God under the aspects of beginning and end and tends to see these as separate also in God's self. Principium and finis, the two aspects under which the human mind thinks of God, are reflected in speech: the truth is that God is both and can be spoken of and at the same time cannot be spoken of. Eriugena is well aware of the need of human beings to be able to speak about the divine nature, but his comments are always checked by the overriding fact of the transcendence of God as infinite and incapable of definition (P. II 586B–587C). "For 'in-finite' is a negation, 'not finite,' and designates that which exceeds all proportion and measure."[26]

How then does partial knowledge of the transcendent find expression in speech about God? According to Eriugena, language is an expression of metaphysical reality, for the whole of the visible world contains symbols that point to God (P. IV 723B; Rom. 1:20). Created effects are the corporeal expression of the incorporeal and can be reflected, however inadequately, in the statements of positive theology. We cannot say anything about God except what the "light of minds has granted us to utter" (P. I 442B), namely, God's self-revelation in theophany as revealed in the scriptures (P. III 633A–634A). The value of positive statements, therefore, cannot be denied because they have scriptural authority. The sacred texts teach what can be said of God, and right reason teaches what should be denied of God.[27] Therefore, although it is clear that nothing should be said about God except that which has been said in the scriptures (P. I 509C, 614C), we should not believe all they say in a proper but in a metaphorical sense (P. I 508D–509B). While God can be "seen" in the effects of creative activity, God simultaneously remains transcendently outside of creation; for this reason all names given to God are transferred from the created realm to the divine nature through the process of metonymy: all can be said of God and all can be denied, an idea that is prominent in the *Divine Names* of the Pseudo-Dionysius (P. I 453B, 480B; *Divine Names* V 8). All things, both like and unlike, can be said of God since God is the source of all things similar and dissimilar (P. I 510D). Because God is the cause of all contraries, everything can be said of God, even things dissimilar. Here, Eriugena follows the Pseudo-Dionysius closely: like symbolism more easily deceives than dissimilar images of the divine, in that the mind cannot take unlike names literally; it immediately understands them to be false or figurative (P. I 512A–B; *Celestial Hierarchy* II 2–3).

And yet Eriugena is not content simply to deny the validity of all affirmations, for negative statements alone have little meaning. He develops what I have elsewhere called the hyperphatic way of speaking about God so familiar from the works of the Pseudo-Dionysius.[28] Since what can be said of God cannot be said properly, either affirmatively or negatively, Eriugena suggests that we use the prefixes *super* or *plus quam*. God is truth; God is not truth; God is more than truth (P. IV 757D–758A). The "more than" does not tell us anything about God but it captures the force of the negative while outwardly remaining positive in construction (P. I 462B–D). In this way, Eriugena preserves the ineffability of the divine nature, not simply because of the human need to "utter the unutterable" but because the divine nature is superessentially unknowable in itself.

Eriugena also follows the Pseudo-Dionysius closely in the method of affirmation and negation. Even the terms "unity," "God," and "Trinity" are subjected to the scrutiny of his penetrating analysis: God is, properly speaking, "plus quam deus" and "plus quam trinitas" (P. I 459D–460A, 456D). In this sense the meaning of "nihil" is made clear for it simply means that God is "plus quam essentia" (P. III 634B–C, 680D). Whatever is said of Trinity and the divine goodness is simply traces and theophanies of the truth (P. II 614C). We can talk of God as unity and Trinity, but only "in order that the religious inclinations of pious minds may have something to think and something to say concerning that which is ineffable and incomprehensible" (P. I 456A). Eriugena, in a close paraphrase of Augustine, observes: "But these are things which are contemplated at a deeper and truer level than they are expressed in speech, and understood more deeply than they are contemplated, and are deeper and truer than they are understood to be; for they pass all understanding" (P. II 614B–C).[29] Thus, while the value of the book of nature is affirmed, it is never completely accurate.

Although Eriugena does not advocate a systematic denial of all things from the lowest to the highest in order to reach an "unknowing" of God as the Pseudo-Dionysius had done, the negation of all statements about God implies an aphairetic method of theology in that the hyperphatic method of theological speech achieves knowledge *that* God is not *what* God is (P. I 487B, 522B; II 572D, 585B; III 634B; IV 779C; V 1010D). All such statements as "God is more than . . . " which encompass both the positive and the negative, are intended to show that while the positive content is not denied neither is it fully affirmed. "When negation denies what the affirmative process has ascribed to the divine origin . . . negation does not simply destroy the meaning of such a statement but makes the statement relative to itself."[30] However, "plus quam" statements are still rooted in the symbolic manifestation of God and do little more than stretch both thought and word as far as they can be stretched in the direction of God. The hyperphatic method of speaking about God has inherent drawbacks since such statements have little content; they are, in a sense, empty. According to Otten's analysis, Eriugena's attempt to say something about God in this way simply clothes the nakedness of God with the "transparent robes of empty superlative predications." Otten senses a conscious decision on Eriugena's part in abandoning formalized methods of speaking about God. She believes that the failure of positive, negative, and hyperphatic speech forces Eriugena to retreat behind the walls of human predication.[31] In this sense, theophany or metaphorical predication becomes the solution to the problem of speech about God because God truly does appear in created effects and can be grasped, at least in a limited fashion, by human understanding. However, to view theophany as superseding all forms of speech about God, in the sense that natura itself is the book wherein God can be read, ignores the fact that human beings need some method of speaking about that which they read. In this sense, hyperphatic speech is most appropriate.

According to Sells, the understanding of God as the ground of reality in terms of "nothing" means that "without a final 'being' to which it can point, language is placed into perpetual movement."[32] However, language, as the verbal expression of the corporeal manifestation of the incorporeal, is never fully rendered meaningless by negation, for creation is the manifestation of God, the father "speaking" the reasons for all things in the Word. The exteriorization of the father's thought in the processio extends to the exteriorization of the effect in human speech. When Eriugena denies something of God, he is not saying that God is not that thing or is nothing but is saying that God is the no-thingness that, paradoxically, is everything. Every negative sentence is, in a sense, "haunted" by God because negations in relation to God are not simply empty phrases.[33] The relentless and insistent manner in which Eriugena questions and casts suspicion on linguistic and cognitive processes leads both word and thought to the very edge of their meaning before a further negation casts them into a new matrix of meaning, which itself will be subject to subsequent transformation. However, language can never escape fully its metaphorical moorings, for neither symbol nor thought can be abandoned fully. In the last analysis, there will always be, between the truth of affirmative and negative statements, a contradiction that cannot be resolved by prefixing each statement with "more than." In this sense, Eriugena's method confronts us with the full force of the inexplicable nature of God as the reconciliation of all opposites, for in God there cannot be opposition, and things in discord cannot be eternal (P. I 453A, 459A). On the epistemological level, as on the ontological level, there will always be a tension between the positive and the negative in relation to the transcendent immanent. Thus, Otten's analysis of language failure is not entirely accurate because a way of speaking cannot be found to describe the ineffable. The immanence and knowability of God through the act of creation must always be denied because God proceeds into knowability while remaining unknowable precisely as other (P. III 644C). The simultaneous motion and rest of God means that God's movement is from God's self towards God's self: "thus going forth into all things in order He makes all things and is made in all things, and returns into Himself, calling all things back to Himself, and while He is made in all things He does not cease to be above all things" (P. III 683B). The Word runs through all things (its diffusion is the cause of all things): "it makes all things and is made in all things, and while in itself it subsists as One, Perfect, and More-than-Perfect, and separate from all things" (P. III 643B). However, even though the epistemological dialectic that results from the simultaneous transcendence and immanence of God means that the tension between the positive and the negative cannot be resolved fully (at least not until that time when God shall be "all in all"), there is always a tendency to favor the transcendent through a negative formulation over the immanent through a positive formulation. According to Sells, Eriugena's use of "theophanic antimonies" (such as "unmanifest manifest") is intended to show that "the negative remains at a higher level."[34] However, the tension between transcendence and immanence cannot be "resolved" through favoring either, for at the very heart of revealed religion is the truth that the transcendent became immanent while remaining transcendent.

I have already shown that on the verbal level, the hypherphatic method of speech about God reconciles the positive and the negative. In the *Periphyseon* Eriugena elaborates a way that can reconcile the dialectic, not on the ontological but on the epistemological level. Knowing God as immanent and not knowing God as transcendent can be reconciled through what Eriugena terms "divine ignorance," a theme that is most commonly associated with the more experiential aspect of "knowing" God through "unknowing." However, although Eriugena does discuss the theme of "unknowing knowing," we do not find him elaborating a theory of attaining to a supernatural unity with God, such as is evident in the *Enneads* of Plotinus or the *Mystical Theology* of the Pseudo-Dionysius. I discuss this point further in chapter 7. According to Eriugena, divine ignorance (which is a Neoplatonic, specifically Plotinian criticism of Aristotle's self-thinking thought),[35] signifies the fact that God is ignorant of God's essence. However, this ignorance is paradoxically true knowledge because it means that God knows that God is none of the things of creation. This statement is the key to the realization that God's ignorance is really an ineffable understanding (P. II 593C, 597C–D). God is unable to know God's essence because it is only by creating itself that the divine essence comes to know itself in something; in itself it is nothing (P. III 689A–B). In this sense, the knowledge God has of God's self is knowledge only through becoming other than God, even though this other is not other than God in God's self. "It follows that we ought not to understand God and the creature as two things distinct from one another, but as one and the same. For both the creature, by subsisting is in God; and God, by manifesting Himself, in a marvelous and ineffable manner creates Himself in the creature, the invisible making Himself visible and the incomprehensible comprehensible and the hidden revealed and the unknown known" (P. III 678C). It follows that if God can become visible and known in created effects to created effects, God can also become known and visible to God's self through the creation of effects. "For the understanding of all things [in God] is the essence of all things . . . God's knowing and God's making are therefore one. For by knowing He makes and by making He knows. . . . For the understanding of all things [in God] is the essence of all things. . . . For the essence of all (things) is nothing but the knowledge of all things in the Divine Wisdom. For in Him we live and move and have our being." (P. II 559A–B) In other words, God realizes God's self as the creative principle of the other and is, therefore, better known by not knowing (*Comm.* I xxv 302B).

Being made in all things, through which God knows God's self in all things, results in the duality, indeed the quadruplicity of natura, and division can be resolved only when the brightness of being is once again dimmed and returns to the superessential darkness of inaccessible light, a theme I discuss in chapter 7. In the meantime, that is, before creation returns to its source, Eriugena argues, God is better known, both by God and by creatures, by not knowing, a familiar sentiment of Plotinus and Augustine, and this "knowledge" is precisely what constitutes true wisdom: to know that God transcends all things and is none of the things that are (P. II 593D, 597D–598A). This idea becomes the key to an understanding of negative theology in the *Periphyseon,* much as it had done in the *Mystical Theology* of the Pseudo-Dionysius. Therefore, to say that God is nihil is true because God is none of the things that are: God is always "more than" (P. II 597C–598A). There is, then, some positive aspect in this kind of knowing, but since it is "unknowing knowing" it is no longer knowledge that can be explained in a systematic fashion: it has no discernible positive content. Eriugena does not (indeed cannot) explain further, because the rules of language, whereby negation becomes affirmation, no longer operate on a strictly logical level. The ineffable mystery of God cannot be encapsulated in positive or negative statements. "He surpasses every intellect and all sensible and intelligible meanings Who is better known by not knowing, of Whom ignorance is true knowledge" (P. I 510B).

Eriugena's continual assertion that God is all things, the one great underlying metaphysical thematic of the *Periphyseon,* is finally shown to be inadequate in the light of the truth that God is none of the things. However, God's knowledge does not end with the admission of ignorance because "He knows that He is none of them, but understands that He excels (them) all by His ineffable essential Power and More-than-Power, and by His incomprehensible Infinity" (P. II 596D). The power of unknowing, which transforms ignorance into knowledge, ensures that Eriugena's "system" does not "crash." The statement that God is none of the things is tempered by the addition: God is "more than" them. For this reason we can say that Eriugena's negative theology is not simply a theory of language based on respect for the ineffable power of God but reflects an understanding of reality that is not only sustained in the immanent manifestation of God but is also constantly straining toward the unknowable transcendent cause above all things.[36] The constant checks and balances in Eriugena's portrayal of the complexity of natura, the affirmations and denials, the reminders that the immanent is also the transcendent and the transcendent immanent, are strong significations that there can never be a "reconciliation" of the perceived tension between the two because that is precisely the way reality is structured. Any fixed points in the human understanding of God are constantly moveable as the rational power of the mind is continuously pushed up to and at times over the limits of its comprehension. And yet the presence of God in all things is one reassurance that speech is, after all, possible.

HUMAN NATURE IN PARADISE

The anthropology of Eriugena is perhaps the most difficult theme in the *Periphyseon*, and his speculations on the subject of human nature are found chiefly, though not exclusively in book IV. We were warned that the fourth book of the *Periphyseon* would enter into more dangerous waters, indeed at times we do find indeed find ourselves in need of a lifeline in the form of the opinion of Augustine, Ambrose, Basil, or Gregory of Nyssa. However, even though the Irishman's anthropology is a difficult subject, it is worth the effort to understand his concept of the constitution, role, and place of human nature in the scheme of *natura* because it is his understanding that it is within human nature that the whole of creation is brought together in an ineffable harmony. Thus far, the themes I have examined in Eriugena's writings could give the impression that the different aspects of his thought can be understood separately; that is not the case. Eriugena's thought forms a complex but unified whole, and nowhere is this more clearly seen than in his understanding of human nature which holds the whole of creation together.

Perhaps the most striking aspect of Eriugena's anthropology in *Periphyseon* book IV is his sustained use of the allegorical method of exegesis of the Genesis text, a text he probes mercilessly in the search for a satisfactory and comprehensive account of the creative activity of the transcendent God.[1] Through his perceptive analysis of selected verses from Genesis 1–3, the various shades of meaning of the creative process are carefully unveiled so as to make possible a full understanding of the role of human nature in the universe. Eriugena's sometimes audacious, sometimes delightful but always meticulous interpretation of the Genesis text does not so much tell a different story as, rearrange the elements of a familiar story so that new perspectives and shades of meaning can be seen there. Book IV of the *Periphyseon* reveals not only his exegetical prowess but also his gift as a skilful navigator. Although his guides to a correct understanding of the events of the sixth day of creation are the eminent authorities Augustine, Gregory of Nyssa, Basil and Ambrose, Eriugena, with his usual gift for originality, does not hesitate to abandon their maps in favor of his own or indeed, at times, to redraw theirs to reveal more nuanced shades of meaning. From the exegetical point of view, Eriugena makes extensive use of St. Paul to clarify his understanding of human nature, especially in relation to its fallen state and the struggle of reason for mastery over sense.

Many fascinating shades of meaning emerge from the Genesis text under the skilful guidance of one of the great masters of Carolingian exegesis; for example, Eriugena postpones the attainment of paradise until the eschaton which is the inevitable conclusion of his location of paradise in human nature itself. Eriugena also argues that the idea of human nature resides in the divine mind, indeed that human nature itself is a primordial cause. Eriugena's understanding of human nature can be seen as a reflection of his understanding of the process of the revelation of God. Just as God became not God through manifestation and self-creation in theophany while remaining God, so in the process of being embodied in the material world, human being becomes not-human through its own self-creation, that is, through its willingness to turn away from its original nature. According to Eriugena, Genesis teaches the return of human nature to its source. Thus, the circularity of his thought is once again revealed: the end clarifies the beginning in relation to created natures. One basic feature of Eriugena's anthropology is its theocentric character, derived no doubt from his reliance on the Greek fathers Basil of Caeserea and Gregory of Nyssa.[2] How Eriugena argues to these conclusions I examine hereafter.

The Genesis Story: Day Six

The importance of the first three chapters of Genesis for Eriugena's anthropology cannot be stressed enough. Even though he may at times digress far from the original text in his search for an understanding of the mystery of human nature and its place in the universe, the Genesis story punctuates book IV at significant points so that the reader is drawn fully into the context of Eriugena's discussion. Such a starting point would not perhaps appeal to some philosophers and theologians today, but during the Carolingian period especially, the study of the sacred texts had assumed a renewed importance. Their relevance, and in particular the text of Genesis, was not only theological "but also involved metaphysics, as well as physics and related disciplines. Genesis was the ultimate heuristic context within which any and all statements about the universe had to be situated."[3]

Eriugena's exegesis of day six of the Genesis story (Gen. 1:24) begins with a complicated argument that ultimately leads to the conclusion that all living things are created in human nature. Throughout the first part of this exegesis of Gen. 1:24, the alumnus takes on the role of a questioning child. His relentless "But why . . . ?" is eventually rewarded when at last the matter is clarified to his satisfaction. In order to demonstrate Eriugena's thought processes at work, during the first part of the following discussion I adhere closely to the text of *Periphyseon* IV.

"Let the earth bring forth the living soul in its genus, cattle and reptiles and the beasts of the field according to their species" (P. IV 744B). "Living soul" in this rendering of the divine precept encompasses the whole of animal reality including human nature, and the nutritor piles up text after text from the scriptures in support of this interpretation. Thus, according to Eriugena's exegesis, human nature, "this greatest and most precious species of animal" is recorded twice in the Genesis story of the sixth day: first under the genus of animal and then as in the image and likeness of God (P. IV 750B–C). Not surprisingly, the alumnus is not entirely happy with the inclusion of human being in the genus animal since human being has dominion over all the animals, forcing the nutritor to examine the constitution of human nature in more detail. His conclusion is that human being shares sensation with the beasts and nutritive forces with reptilian life forms. "Man participates in these together with all other animals, and conversely all the other animals participate in them in common with him" (P. IV 752C). Thus, since human nature is in all animals and all animals are in human nature, human nature is included in the genus animal. However, that cannot be the end of the story because "the admirable and absolutely ineffable constitution" of human nature created in the image and likeness of God means that human being transcends all animals (P. IV 752C). In order to resolve this dilemma, Eriugena has recourse to a familiar dialectical method: human nature is animal in so far as its lower nature is concerned and human nature is not animal in so far as it shares its higher nature with the angels. Thus, the definition of human nature as a rational, mortal, risible animal as given in book I (444B) is transformed through the dialectical understanding that human nature cannot be defined, a theme I discuss in greater detail in chapter 6 in relation to what has been called Eriugena's negative anthropology. This solution, however, does not satisfy the alumnus. "I still do not see how one and the same man can, as this discussion seeks to demonstrate, be, and yet not be, an animal; possess, and yet not possess, animality; be, and yet not be, flesh, be, and yet not be, spirit" (P. IV 755A). Here the nutritor sharpens his focus, stating with Maximus that human nature is the "container" of all creation (P. IV 755B, 760A, 763D–764A, 773D); he also calls human nature the "workshop" of all (P. V 893C).[4] Human nature is animal because it consists of body, living being, and sensible being; it is celestial because it is both rational and intellectual being (P. IV 755B, 735D–736A). Human nature is animal through freedom and is spiritual through grace (P. IV 756A). Its dual aspect is a result of the fall from grace through the sin of Adam and Eve; in its animality, it turns to temporal and corruptible things, toward evil, and in its spiritual nature, it turns away from the world and its fleshy nature toward good (P. IV 756A–B). Thus, since human nature is both body and spirit, in it "all creatures visible and invisible . . . the whole spread of creation is understood to inhere" (P. IV 763D). The Pauline statement "it is sown an animal body; it will rise a spiritual body" (1 Cor. 15:44) is here used to explain the dual nature of human beings (P. IV 760C, 764A; II 584C). Therefore, we can say that God placed human nature in the genus animal because God wanted to create every creature in human nature (P. IV 764B). But how can the rational and the irrational be included in the same genus—surely this is contradictory? The nutritor's answer to this question is that the distinction between rational and irrational animality is one of difference, not one of contradiction, because according to the rules of logic, contradictory statements of the same subject (the genus animal) cannot both be true (P. IV 756D). The astute alumnus then asks why the nutritor has allowed such statements to be made about human nature and denied to the genus animal (P. IV 757B–C). Here, after so much rational labor and logical investigation, the reason is given as to why human nature is special: it alone is made in the image of God. Just as mutually adverse predicates can be said of the divine nature, such predicates can also be said of the image of that nature, a hint of what is to come in relation to Eriugena's conception of the attributes of the image of the divine exemplar (P. IV 758B). The whole of creation that is created in human nature includes not only sensible, corporeal realities but also intelligible, celestial realities. As I will show, Eriugena will argue that human nature, as it was intended to be, enjoyed the same status as the angelic intellects (P. IV 774B).[5]

But would human nature have remained animal if it had not sinned? In answer to this question, Eriugena argues that in the creation of human nature, animal nature is not regarded as a punishment for disobedience of the divine precept. The fault leveled against human nature concerns its irrational action in turning toward the material through "dishonoring the natural dignity" of its nature by improper activity (P. IV 762A). Thus, human nature would have been animal even without sin: "for it was not sin but nature which made an animal of him" (P. IV 763A). Why, then, did God create human nature in the genus animal, a genus in which human is not destined to remain, since when the world perishes, all animality will perish with it? (P. IV 763B). Eriugena's answer: "He wished so to fashion him that there might be one among the animals in which His image was expressly manifested" (P. IV 763C).

Angels in Paradise

Thus far it would appear that Eriugena is saying that even angels are created in human nature, so how does he argue to this seemingly audacious point?

First of all, there are two ways of looking at human nature: its presently actualized reality and its natural potency, that is, in itself in the world and in its
reason in the Word (P. IV 770C–771A). In its cause, human nature is eternal,
causal, simple, and created as intelligible; in itself, it is temporal, caused, subject to accident, and generated among effects. Thus, the same thing can be
thought of as two since it can be known in its effects and in its causes (P. IV
771A–704B). Given the fact that human nature is divided, that it has been
sundered from its eternal, intelligible self, it would perhaps have been better,
as the alumnus points out, if God had created all things in angelic rather than
in human nature. The nutritor is not swayed by the generally accepted status
of the angels as superior, and he explains that despite the strong similarity that
exists between the human and celestial (a similarity that is based on the fact
that both are rational, intelligible creatures), some things exist in human nature that do not exist in angelic nature: the five senses, the ideas of sensible
objects, and reason's inquiry into the nature of things. In short, all that is
not innate in human nature, that is, all that has been added to human nature
through the fall from grace, is not possessed by the angelic intellect (P. IV
773B). Thus, human nature becomes a kind of intermediary between corporeal and spiritual realities, between intellect and sense, which are gathered
into one in it (P. V 893C; P. II 529D–530C). We can conclude, then, that human
nature both is and is not what it was intended to be.

What kind of creation of human nature took place on the sixth day as related in Genesis? What kind of creation was human nature before it took on its
earthly, corporeal existence? According to Eriugena's account, which relies
heavily on Gregory of Nyssa's *On the Making of Man*, there were two creations
in relation to human nature: the first, in which the body and soul were created together (P. II 582A–B), and the second, whereby human being is born
into this world.[6] Thus, to speak about human nature as it was intended to be
is to speak of its immutability; that which is mutable has been added through
the process of generation and does not pertain to its true nature, which is spiritual (P. IV 800D–801D). It is, of course, the spiritual, changeless body that
bears the likeness of God (P. IV 802A–B). However, as the alumnus points out,
this account of the dual creation of human nature, which has a scriptural origin in the two accounts of creation in Genesis (1:26 and 2:7; P. IV 833C–
834A), creates the difficult problem of reconciling it with the teaching of
Augustine. Here, once again, we have an instance of Eriugena as intermediary between Eastern and Western ideas, and the reconciliation of Augustine
and Gregory of Nyssa on this point demands attention to detail. Eriugena
argues that it is not sufficient to say that the corporeal body that was added
in Gregory of Nyssa's account is the animal body discussed in the account of
Augustine and that Augustine simply omitted mention of the spiritual body
created initially in the image of God (P. IV 804D–805B). Rather, long quotations from Augustine's writings are brought into the text to demonstrate that

the body that Augustine had called "animal" is actually praised and blessed as spiritual. In fact, this conclusion concurs with Eriugena's own portrayal of human nature as having been created in the genus animal. The ultimate solution to the problem of reconciling Eastern and Western authorities on the question of two creations lies in Eriugena's repeated assertion that both were simultaneous: there was no interval of time between the first and the second creation (P. IV 807B–C). As I will show, this means that human nature sinned as soon as it was created; it was not, therefore, in paradise in its original creation. I discuss further consequences of this remarkable idea hereafter.

Thus far, we have established that in relation to human nature, there were two creations, that originally human nature was of the same status as the angels, and that all things were created in it. In relation to Eriugena's explanation of this last point some of the most fascinating and difficult aspects of his thought are revealed.

Ontology and Intelligibility

In answering the question of how all things were created and, more important, are sustained in human nature Eriugena shows himself to be a true idealist, although the difficulties involved in clarifying this concept are numerous (and are outlined at P. IV 764C–765B). Eriugena begins this discussion in a most unexpected place with a strong statement of important epistemic consequence: "everything which is known by the intellect or the reason or imagined by the sense can somehow be created and produced in the knower" (P. IV 756C). This statement marks a very definite shift from exegetical problems of ontology and creation to problems of knowledge and the relationship between ontology and intelligibility. It also involves a change in the role of the alumnus, who assumes the role of nutritor for the first part of the discussion that follows. In order to explain Eriugena's comments on this difficult theme one must first of all recall some key texts. Knowledge presupposes a unity of knower and known: "whatever the intellect shall have been able to comprehend, that it itself becomes" (P. I 449D–450A). According to the fourth mode of being and non-being: "only those things which are contemplated by the intellect alone truly are" (P. I 445B). The central idea in relation to the creative activity of the triune God, that the true essence of all things resides in their causes, situates the substance of realities in the divine intellect. However, Eriugena expands this particular idea to include not only the divine mind but also the human knower. How does he argue to this conclusion? The human ability to analyze and collect into unity the various aspects of natura results in knowledge of external things being born in the mind. In explanation of the relationship between the thing itself and the concept of the thing in the mind, Eriugena relies on Augustine (*On the Trinity* IX, 9): the replicas of sensible things in the mind are better than the actuality of those things (P. IV 766A). Therefore, that which understands is better than that which is understood, which means that the knowledge of all things in divine wisdom is superior to the things of which it is the knowledge (P. IV 766B). Thus far, Eriugena's conclusion is not in the least surprising. However, the linking of knowledge and being in relation to created minds produces a surprising result. In positing a hierarchical structure in relation to knowledge and intelligibility Eriugena states: "not only every nature which has a concept of that which follows it is better and superior, but also the concept itself, through the dignity of the nature in which it resides, greatly excels the object of which it is the concept" (P. IV 766B). The outcome of this discussion is that the created trinity of human mind, skill, and the mind's discipline are contained in the mind of God and that this concept of the human mind and the mind itself are one and the same (P. IV 768A). From this point Eriugena has little difficulty in stating that the substantial definition of human nature is an intellectual concept in the mind of God; the accidental definition of human nature is rational, mortal animal (P. IV 768B–C).[7] The true substance of human nature is "nothing else but the concept of him in the Mind of his Artificer, Who knew all things in Himself before they were made; and that very knowledge is the true and only substance of the things known, since it is in that knowledge that they are most perfectly created and eternally and immutably subsist" (P. IV 768B); this idea is also prominent in Eckhart's thought (see the vernacular sermon *Ave, gratia plena*). However, that the substance of human nature should reside in the mind of God is not a terribly audacious conclusion, given the general focus of Eriugena's thought in terms of God as the essence of all things. Where it does create problems is in relation to the knowledge human nature can have of itself; I discuss this topic hereafter in relation to Eriugena's negative anthropology. Thus, the definition derived from Genesis and so vigorously defended in Eriugena's allegorical exegesis of that text is finally shown to be inadequate. It is set alongside a new definition that does not do away with the old but supersedes it, in that the former definition defines human nature in terms of the attributes acquired through the generation of the substance.

Having clarified the definition of human nature to the satisfaction of the alumnus, the nutritor prepares to deliver the final argument in favor of the idea that in the human mind a concept exists of all that it understands (P. IV 768C–D). The rationale for this argument depends not immediately on the resemblance of the image to the exemplar but on the fact that human nature was given dominion over all living reality in the world. According to Eriugena, the Genesis text on Adam naming all creatures (2:19) is a clear indication that Adam must have understood all things in order to name them (P. IV 769A).

For no substance has been created which is not understood to subsist in him . . . which either is not naturally in him or of which he cannot have the concept; and the concept of the things which are contained within him excels the things of which it is the concept by so much as the nature in which it is constituted excels. . . . Therefore, it is also rightly understood that the things of which the concepts are innate in human nature have their substance in their concepts. For where they have the better knowledge of themselves, there they must be considered to enjoy the truer existence." (P. IV 773D–774A)

Thus the concept of nature that is created in the human mind is the substance of nature itself, just as in the divine mind is the substance of the whole created universe (P. IV 769A–B). This is, despite the declaration of the alumnus to the contrary, one remarkable concept, and it is remarkable because we find here the ontological significance of intelligibility. The human mind functions in similar fashion to the divine mind, in terms of it being the substance of the things it can know, and in a sense becomes a primordial cause.[8]

However, Eriugena does not close the discussion here, for in the context of the question as to how all things were created in human nature when it was created after all other things on the sixth day of creation, he argues that the human mind actually creates the things of which it has the concept. Of course, solutions to questions about human nature do not come easily in this particular book of the *Periphyseon*, and Eriugena begins this discussion with a difficult passage concerning human nature's knowledge of itself.

> I think I should be right in saying that where there is one thing that understands and another that is understood, and where that which understands is of a better nature than that which is understood, the understanding mind or the perceiving sense is prior to the thing which is understood or perceived. But where the things themselves understand themselves . . . I do not see what kind of precedence there can be. Although I know that I am, my knowledge of myself is not prior to myself because I and the knowledge by which I know myself are not two different things: if I did not know that I was I would not be ignorant that I did not know that I was: therefore whether I know or do not know that I am I shall not be without the knowledge: for there will remain the knowledge of my ignorance. And if everything which is able to know that it does not know itself cannot be ignorant of the fact that it is . . . it follows that absolutely everything has existence which knows that it is or knows that it does not know that it is. (P. IV 776B)

In order to explain how the intelligible concept in the mind is prior to intelligible or sensible realities, Eriugena modifies the statement that the knower is better than the known: the knower is prior to the known, not in time but ontologically. However, in the case of human beings, knowledge of the self and the self are not two different things: knowledge of self is not prior to the self, a fact which is further complicated by the notion that the human subject is ignorant of its true substance since that remains hidden in the mind of God. Thus it would seem that the logical difficulty of the concept being prior to the reality has been immeasurably complicated by the fact of human ignorance, a difficulty to which Eriugena will turn his attention in a few moments. Let me first comment on the text quoted above which has been the subject of some scholarly analysis. In a seminal article on this subject, Brian Stock argued that Eriugena's *cogito* was a link between Augustine's affirmation of individual existence and Descartes's *cogito*.[9] However, with Otten, I do not believe that Eriugena's text establishes "a modern concept of individuality" or that he was trying to prove human existence as Brian Stock claimed he was.[10] Human knowing, which is inherently deficient and incapacitated as a result of the fall, simply cannot define itself: it can know only that it is, not what it is. According to Eriugena's understanding, to know that one is is self-evident; those who do not know that they are are either not human or else they must be dead (P. IV 776C). Indeed, human nature will never know itself completely, even in its final state of restoration to its cause, since that would presume, most audaciously, that it will know the mind of God. However, Eriugena does not dwell on this issue because his tactic here is leading to a resolution of the problem of the human mind creating the things of which it has the concept. The next point to clarify concerns when human being received knowledge of itself: was it in the primordial causes or through the generative process? The answer is, not surprisingly, in both: general knowledge comes secretly through the causes, while specific knowledge comes openly in the effects (P. IV 776B). For Eriugena, as for Gregory of Nyssa, generation in the world in a corporeal body obscures the knowing capacity of human nature as it was intended to be. "For most mighty and most wretched was that Fall in which our nature lost the knowledge and the wisdom which had been planted in her, and lapsed into a profound ignorance of herself and her Creator" (P. IV 777C–D). Before the fall, it would appear that human nature possessed the fullest knowledge of all essences and natures. Just as the creative wisdom of the Word beholds all things before they are made, and that knowledge is their eternal, immutable, and primary causal essence, "so the created wisdom, which is human nature, knows all things which are made in it before they are made, and that very knowledge of the things which are known before they are made is their true and indestructible essence" (P. IV 779A). Eriugena concludes that just as the divine intellect is prior to all things, so too the intellectual knowledge of the soul is prior to all the things that it knows. This means that one and the same essence can be contemplated under two aspects: in the causes in which it passes all understanding and in the effects in which it is known that it is. Thus it is that the original problem is solved: there was no creature before human nature, since it is prior to all that was created with it, in it, or below it (P. IV 779D).

The lengths to which Eriugena has goes in defense of the idea that all things were created in human nature reveals some rather surprising results along the way, not least of which is the causal capacity of human nature itself. In fact, he is even prepared to state that there was "no creature, either visible or invisible before the creation of man . . . man's creation is prior to those things which were created with it . . . that is to say the celestial essences" (P. IV 779D). That human nature is equal in status to angelic nature is a frequently recurring theme in the *Periphyseon*, since before the fall, Eriugena believes, they were identical (P. II 575A).[11] Eriugena's words are strong here, contrary to what many believe is stated in the Genesis text; "by no law of creation or method of precedence can it rightly be believed or understood that the angel is prior to man" (P. IV 780D–781A). If we follow Augustine's exegesis of Genesis 1:1, 1:3, and 1:4–5 concerning the creation of the celestial intelligences on the first intelligible day and the creation of human nature on the sixth intelligible day, how can we state that human nature is prior to angel? Eriugena's answer to this problem simply augments the Augustinian exegesis of the *fiat lux* that had signified the creation of angels. Because the creation of angels is not specific ("Let there be light"), "we may understand that the creation of the substance of man, no less than that of angel, is to be inferred in the creation of light" (P. IV 782A–B). Thus, the reason why human nature is related as having been created on the sixth day as the conclusion of the creative process is to demonstrate that all that was previously created is universally understood in human nature. If 'the story had told of the creation of human nature first, everything in creation would appear to be outside human nature, and that cannot be the case (P. IV 782C–783A; V 893C).

The most important idea to emerge from Eriugena's discussion of the creation of human nature thus far in *Periphyseon* book IV is that understanding creates and human nature is nothing other than its intellection. This thesis is expressed in a remarkable passage in which Eriugena relates what happens when two people enter into a discussion together: "each of us is created in the other: for when I understand what you understand I am made in your understanding, and in a certain way that cannot be described I am created in you" (P. IV 780B–C). And what precisely is human intellection? It is nothing else but the image of God within human nature (P. IV 780C).

In the Image of God

Eriugena's exegesis of Genesis 1:26–27 begins with a brief recapitulation of the creative role of the Trinity (Gen. 1:1–3), and the whole first part of the ensuing discussion, which includes some very lengthy quotations from Gregory of Nyssa's *On the Making of Man*, is put in the mouth of the alumnus (P. IV 786D–799A). The relationship of image to exemplar is an interesting aspect of Eriugena's thought, and he relies chiefly on Gregory of Nyssa in the assertion that the image is perfectly image except in subject (P. II 585A), although the true image of God is the Word (P. II 580A); human nature is simply made in the image and likeness of God, that is, in the Word. "Where the image is created, there the Primal Exemplar of which it is the image is most expressly revealed" (P. IV 786C; II 585A).

The first question to be clarified is whether human nature, composed of body and soul, is wholly or partly made in the image of God. The answer to this question, which concludes that the whole image subsists in the whole animal, rests on the fundamental assertion that God is beyond all things and in all things (P. IV 759A–B). Eriugena begins, following Augustine, that human nature is neither bodily nor spiritually but intelligibly in the image of God (P. IV 786D–787A). While the soul can be said to possess certain movements—intellect, reason, interior sense, exterior sense, and vital motion—it is, at the same time, simple and whole; it is not a unity of parts. It is rather, by "a certain wonderful and intelligible division that man is divided into two parts" (P. IV 754A–B). Relying on Gregory of Nyssa, Eriugena states that soul is "the most simple, the most indivisible and the most impartible essence and is not lesser in her minor offices nor magnified in her greater offices nor is she greatest in her greatest offices, but in all she is equal of herself" (P. IV 787D–788A, 824C–825C). Thus, the whole soul is made in the image of God: the mind is in the true image of God, reason (the material life principle) is the image of the image, and matter is the second image of the image. Even though it is primarily in the mind that human nature is made in the image of God (P. IV 790C–D), Eriugena also finds an exalted place for the other parts of human nature.

The second question to clarify is what kind of image is present in human nature. Eriugena, inspired by Augustine and Gregory of Nyssa, is clear that the image of the divine nature in human nature is trinitarian, both universally as essence, power, and operation and also particularly in relation to each aspect (P. II 568A–B). Human nature expresses the image of the trinity through its constitution as essence (being), power (willing), and operation (knowing—or intellect, reason, and sense), that is, father, son, and spirit (P. II 506B, 566D–568A, 569B, 575D; IV 825C; V 941D–942A, 953A).

Of the five parts of the soul, intellect, reason, sense, body, and life principle, only the first three, the "inner man" are made in the image of God; body and life principle, the "outer man" were added after the fall (P. II 570D–571B; 2 Cor. 4:16). It is with regard to intellect, reason, and interior sense that Eriugena sets down his understanding of the true constitution of human nature and its role as knower. Intellect, which is unknowable in itself, is the part of human nature that is capable of transcending itself; continuously, as in the Pseudo-Dionysius and Maximus the Confessor, it revolves around the unknown God beyond all things (P. II 570A–B, 572C–D, 577B, 585B). Reason, the form of intellect made manifest, is concerned with the principles of things and defines the unknown God as the cause of all created reality (P. II 570C, 573A).

Interior sense, which is coessential with intellect and reason, is concerned with the effects of the primordial causes and attains to knowledge of sensible things (P. II 570C, 573A–B). Exterior sense is the link between body and soul (P. II 569A–570A).[12] This tripartite division of soul in human nature, while not original to Eriugena, is used by him to the greatest effect in the sense that intellect remains somehow above the rest of its nature despite the fall and the banishment from paradise. In reality, the true nature of soul extends beyond all creatureliness and "revolves about its Creator in an eternal and intelligible motion" (P. IV 754C) just as the angelic intellects are in eternal circular motion around God (P. IV 773C–D). According to Eriugena, the essential being of the soul "is not other than her substantial motion" (P. II 574B). I discuss the ability of human nature to transcend itself in relation to the ascent to God in chapter 7, but let me say here that this capacity (exemplified by the Dionysian prayer for Timothy, which is quoted on a number of occasions by Eriugena) is the direct result of the image of God within, and in this sense, human nature truly reflects its divine exemplar in that while it is embodied, it remains a spiritual essence.

Thus Eriugena finds the foundation for his continual assertions of the dignity of human nature. Human nature exists simultaneously in God's mind and as an effect; in this sense, we can say that God is in the creature and the creature is in God (P. III 678C). The superiority and dominion human nature enjoys over all the rest of creation is, therefore, rightly deserved and is only slightly tarnished by the sin of Adam and Eve. The Eriugenian conception of the dignity of human nature is a constant theme in *Periphyseon* book IV. Despite the awful consequences of the sin of disobedience on the part of Adam and Eve, the true nature of the soul as in the image of the transcendent God is never fully concealed. And yet Eriugena makes one further, almost unthinkable, amendment to his concept of human nature as having been created in the image of God. Toward the end of *Periphyseon* book V, in the context of a discussion of the return of all things to God, he reinterprets the significance of human nature as image: "if he keep My commandment, he may become Our image and likeness" (1013C). Thus, even this most fundamental of concepts is given an eschatological dimension, one further proof that for Eriugena, an understanding of the beginning simply clarifies the end.

bliss said to have been enjoyed by human nature in paradise is subject to a most unusual interpretation by Eriugena because he ultimately argues that human nature did not enjoy a state of perfection because it turned from God as soon as it was created. Thus the logic of the earlier argument that God made human nature in the genus animal becomes clear: "because He foresaw that he would come to live as an animal and that he would fall from the beauty and dignity of the divine image into a life of irrational animal passion" (P. IV 807B). Following Gregory of Nyssa, Eriugena adheres to the view that in God's creation of human nature, God also created the consequences of sin even before the sin occurred, since it is an undeniable fact that God created all things simultaneously (P. IV 807C).[2] God's foreknowledge, which ultimately cannot be questioned, is used to explain away certain difficulties that arise in relation to the two creations of human nature. The consequences of sin, as I will show, are understood to precede the actual deed of sin. Thus, Eriugena inverts the temporal order of the events as related in Genesis 1.[3] The explanation for this interpretation is based on the general fact that in God there is no time—temporal sequences are a result of the mutability of human thought—for the whole of creation was simultaneous. There is nothing before or after God, no past or future, nor even the passage between past and future, "for to Him all things are at once present" (P. IV 808A). In this way Eriugena will argue that sin belongs to human categories, not to God. Thus, he can assert quite confidently that human beings were not in paradise for any time before the fall, for if they had stayed there, they "would have achieved some perfection" (P. IV 809B–C, 808A–B, 810 B–C, 838B). This loss of historical underpinnings makes Eriugena's exegesis of the Genesis text uniquely his own; in fact, he states that the text itself does not record a temporal interval between creation and the fall. How, then, does this account by the Irish exegete relate to the story of creation in Genesis itself and its interpretation by other exegetes?

The frequent references to the fall in the *Periphyseon* are often couched in terms that evoke the fall of Sophia in the Gnostic myth (Irenaeus *Against Heresies* I, 2.2) and the fall of the soul from the One (through *tolma*) in the *Enneads* of Plotinus (VI 9', 9, 33–38). "[T]hrough the accident of its transgression of the divine command whereby it became forgetful both of itself and its creator the mind is born unskilled and unwise" (P. IV 767C, 761A, 777C–D). Ignorance of God, then, is one consequence of human nature turning away from God into the darkness of ignorance (*Hom.* XII 290A; P. IV 761A; V 852A). For Eriugena, the fall is considered an irrational, inexplicable movement, a movement that is outside human nature because it entails going against and abandoning "the more exalted beauty of the Divine image" (P. IV 762B; V 874D). However, despite the bleak consequences of human nature turning to itself away from God, Eriugena tells us that human nature did not wish to sin; indeed he states, more startlingly, that its creator did not wish to punish it, a topic I discuss hereafter. Human nature was deceived and blinded by its own depraved will, by the wrong use of the beauty of material objects, which is the tasting of forbidden fruit bringing death to the soul (P. IV 849B; *Enn.* III 5, 1; V 5, 12). However, even despite its shortcomings, human nature should not be viewed in a negative way (P. IV 761A, 849B); rather, it should be viewed positively in the light of its primal creation as it was established before the fall in the image of God, in "a condition in which she eludes in a mysterious way, through the ineffable dignity of her nature, every bodily sense and all mortal thought" (P. IV 760D–761A). For Eriugena, sin is the turning away from the creator, abandoning the image of God to become like irrational, mortal animals (P. IV 761A, 817D, 846A). Adam's sin was that he fell in love with "woman" (sense) and abandoned God; in other words, he was lured by the attraction of the beauty of the senses and in doing so turned away from his intellectual principle. Eriugena makes frequent use of the allegorical interpretation of Adam as reason and Eve as sense, derived most likely from Philo of Alexandria through Ambrose of Milan (P. II 541A; IV 813B–C, 815C–D, and 833A–B; *On the Making of the World* 165). While this is not a particularly flattering identification in the light of contemporary feminist theology, Eriugena is clear that both together make up human nature (P. IV 833B). Woman was not created simply for assistance in the process of mortal generation, because the image of God in which the whole of human nature was made was free from all sexuality. Because God foresaw that human nature would not wish to remain in the dignity of its natural state, God added the sexual division to its mortal nature (P. IV 846A–B). "Let us make woman for it is not good that man should be alone" (Gen. 2:18) is interpreted as God's ironic statement that *man* did not wish to remain alone, simple, and perfect in his natural dignity as the image of God but wished to propagate like the animals (P. IV 846B–C).[4] On examining the various texts in the *Periphyseon* dealing with the fall, one can detect some ambiguity in Eriugena's account: the soul was deceived and the fall was accidental, not natural; human nature knowingly abandoned the image of its creator. Did human nature turn willingly from God, or was it accidental? Eriugena eventually argues, in the light of the double creation of human nature, that sin is foreign to the innate rationality of human nature, a stance that enables him to "salvage," at least partly, the dignity of human nature notwithstanding its moment of irrationality.

In his exegesis of the banishment of Adam and Eve from paradise, Eriugena paints a very vivid picture of God's rebuke to Adam, Eve, and the serpent and extrapolates on the original text of Genesis 3:9–24 by putting a lengthy passage into the mouth of God. Adam's defense, that the woman was to blame, is sharply dismissed by God: "such a shift of guilt is no defence but rather an aggravation of the offence" (P. IV 846D). Similarly, Eve is chastised for attempting to transfer her guilt to the serpent (P. IV 847B–848A). However, in the banishment from paradise, God does not "curse" Adam and Eve (mind and interior sense) but curses only the serpent (irrational, corporeal sense), for

"God does not curse the things which He made, but blesses them; and mind and sense are both creations of God" (P. IV 848C). But carnal delight, the wrong use of earthly beauty and material things, is severely dealt with by God since this was not created by God (P. IV 848C–D). Here again, we see Eriugena following through on his fundamental belief that human nature, as the image of God, is intrinsically good.

In the early part of his exegesis of the Genesis text in relation to the fall, Eriugena concentrates on the implication of sin specifically in terms of the creation of male and female. Considered in its correct substantial fashion, male and female are not the names of human nature but are the result of its further division through disobedience. Eriugena's interpretation of the primal creation, in which he follows Gregory of Nyssa closely, states that human nature was created whole, without further division (P. II 537C, 542C–543B). The irrational movement of sin created dissimilarity from the exemplar and the formlessness of imperfection in the further division of its whole nature into two parts (P. II 598B; IV 743A; V 874D). According to Eriugena, all responsibility for the fall rests with human nature, including the making of its corporeal body, an idea derived from Gregory of Nyssa's interpretation of Genesis 3:7. Human nature makes a "mortal mansion" for itself from earthly matter; the fig leaves with which human nature covered its nakedness were made by itself and hide the divine image that is its natural substance (P. II 583C). "For as those leaves cast a shadow (and) shut out the rays of the sun, so our bodies both cast upon our souls the darkness of ignorance and keep out the knowledge of the truth" (P. II 583C). However, here once again, Eriugena takes liberties with the reading of the text of Genesis, for he notes that the covering of its body with fig leaves is recorded out of sequence in Genesis, for this action is a consequence of sin. If paradise is human nature itself in the image of God, as I will show hereafter, as soon as it sinned it fell away, lost the divine image, and was banished from paradise, that is, was separated from its true nature (P. IV 838A). Because the body is mortal and corruptible, it cannot have been made by God but through the irrational motions of the human soul. But what happened to its first body? According to Eriugena, the first incorruptible body of human nature is still hidden in the "secret recesses of nature" (P. II 584C).

This fundamental optimism in Eriugena's conception of human nature does not always rest easily with his frequent portrayals of that nature in comparison with its former status. In the primal creation it was blessed, rich, and eternal and had everlasting life, was wise, spiritual, and heavenly and had eternal youth, and was happy, saved, and prudent; now it is wretched, needy, temporal, mortal, foolish, animal, and earthly and will grow old and is lost and prodigal (P. IV 862B; II 540A). However, because of his fundamental belief in the goodness of human nature as in the image of God, Eriugena argues that the creator did not wish to punish it; God simply added a corporeal body through which the fault of Adam and Eve might be purged (P. IV 761A). Human nature was not banished from paradise into the world through God's anger or through revenge but as a kind of "ineffable teaching and incomprehensible clemency" (P. II 540B). Sexuality, then, and the division it signifies in its movement from wholeness, is part payment for the sin of disobedience.[5] However, despite the rather negative tone Eriugena adopts when speaking about the division into the sexes and human nature's adoption of a method of propagation that is like that of the beasts, he does say that sex is not necessarily a bad thing, indeed it cannot be so because it was created by God (P. IV 799C). Human nature may have created its own body but it did not make the initial division into the sexes; that was added by God in order to facilitate generation. Thus, while we must understand sexual division as a deviation from the wholeness in which human nature was originally created and as a penalty for transgression, marriage and procreation should not be regarded in a bad light (P. IV 846D–847A).

Sense and Reason: The Struggle for Supremacy

In the latter part of his exegesis of Genesis 3:15–16 Eriugena turns his attention to a much more important consequence of the fall: the damage caused to the natural constitution of human nature by the addition of a corporeal body. This aspect of human nature's earthly embodiment concerns the struggle of reason to overcome its earthly passions in order to come to a sure and true knowledge of itself, of God, and of the whole of natura. One boundary to complete knowledge which Eriugena confronts is that human nature cannot know what it is, only that it is; this conclusion depends on three fundamental principles. First, the knower is greater than the known; second, all intellects are defined by what is above them; and third, a substantial definition of any ousia is impossible given that its essence resides in the divine mind. Thus, following Gregory of Nyssa, he argues that the accidents and additions to human nature show that it is, but this remains a circumstantial definition only because the human image of the divine essence "is not bound by any fixed limit any more than the Divine Essence in Whose image it is made" (P. IV 772A). Since definition places the limitation of finitude on an entity, it follows that because human nature is not finite (its essence resides in the eternal Word), it cannot be defined substantially. The invisible and incomprehensible creator of human nature created the image of God fully in that nature; that means the image of the incomprehensible must also be incomprehensible; any dissimilarity to be found between exemplar and image is not from nature but is accidental as a result of sin (P. II 598B). Following Gregory of Nyssa, Eriugena declares that if human nature could know what it was, it would no longer be an image of God because all that is said of the exemplar can also be said of the image (P. II 589B; IV 778A–B, 788D). Just as God transcends all things by the excellence of God's essence, the image of God transcends all things in both dignity and in grace (P. IV 764B; II 585B–C). Therefore, concludes Eriugena, human nature can know that it is but not what it is (P. I 443B; II 585B; IV 771A–C). As a created essence, human nature can understand: that it is, that it can understand that it is, and that it does understand that it is (P. I 490B). Ultimately, since human nature is a concept in the mind of God, it remains a mystery to itself just as God is a mystery to God's self (P. IV 768B). Immediately we can see that human nature has a very fundamental problem: if it cannot define what it is, and if it cannot know itself, how will it come to a sure knowledge of the rest of natura, which is created in it? In a very fundamental sense, human self-awareness is incomplete because of the tension that exists between the knowledge that it is and the ignorance of what it is.

How, then, does Eriugena extricate himself from this hopeless situation? He attempts to resolve the problem of human ignorance of itself in the same way as he had resolved the problem of God's ignorance of God's self. Just as God's ignorance can be shown to be wisdom, so too "the ignorance in it of what it is is more praiseworthy than the knowledge that it is, just as the negation of God accords better and more suitably with the praise of His Nature than the affirmation" (P. IV 771C). However, ignorance in God could be regarded as wisdom in that it was actually the knowledge that God is above all things; the same proviso cannot be made in relation to human nature because its ignorance of itself does not constitute another form of knowledge. Thus, ignorance and knowledge in human nature admit of an ambiguous relationship: human nature is made ignorant of God after the fall but even in its restored state, human nature will also be ignorant of God and will, therefore, remain ignorant of itself (*Hom.* XII 290A). The ignorance that results from the not-knowing of human nature by itself is not a theme that is developed in the *Periphyseon;* indeed it cannot be since even without sin, human nature would be able to see God not by its own strength but only through divine grace, although even then the highest knowledge or vision of God is mediated through theophany. "Human nature, even if it did not sin, could not of its own proper resources shine; for according to its nature it is not light but partakes of light" (*Hom.* XIII 290C).[6] "For there appears to be no effective means whereby man's knowledge arising from his transcendence of the boundaries of finite knowledge can be distinguished in any way from the ignorance which is indicative of the loss of the knowledge he was entitled to and was intended to have at his disposal."[7] Yet, even here, we can detect an ambiguity in Eriugena's conception of knowledge of God before the fall, during this life, and in the restoration of all things to God, a point I discuss further in chapter 7.

In the fall from intelligibility, from its true nature, Eriugena conceives of human nature moving from unity to become other than its true self. Just as

God becomes not God through the creative process, so too human nature becomes not human nature when it makes itself a mortal body and becomes visible in sensible reality. Just as God remains hidden in otherness, so too human nature remains hidden in otherness, hidden in its corporeality.[8] By abandoning the perfection of its intellectual, circular movement around God, the human intellect loses its capacity to contemplate creation in the unity of the primordial causes. Through reasoning dialectically, which in a sense "spells out" the details of the fragmentation of natura, the human mode of knowing is incapacitated.[9] The endeavor of human rationality, then, consists of reversing the consequences of the fall through turning back to God, and it does this through the mastery of reason over sense. How does Eriugena reach this conclusion?

He begins with a most interesting interpretation of Genesis 3:15, the enmity created between the woman and her seed and the serpent and its seed. "Woman," the corporeal sense in human nature, is corrupted by the serpent, which is "lustful indulgence in material beauty." The seed of woman "is the perfect, natural and multiple knowledge of visible things, free from all error" (P. IV 851A–B). In good and righteous people, their "woman" is not deceived by the beauty of material realities: they can distinguish between good and evil assisted by the "stronger woman" who is the Word of God (P. IV 853B–C). But they must always take care because the "heel of the woman," the fantasies of sensible things, can always be attacked by the serpent through the wrong use of the senses.

The "curse" of Eve (Gen. 3:16), traditionally understood to relate to the consequences of painful labor in childbirth as a result of the fall, is brought into Eriugena's framework of argumentation in support of his portrayal of the disability suffered by reason through the fall. In a most original interpretation, Eriugena suggests that through sorrows and labor, that is, through hard work in study, reason can come to a true understanding of the things of natura, that is, metaphorical "sons" (P. IV 855A–B). The loss of the most pure manner of contemplating reality demands, therefore, a high price in terms of reason's labor toward understanding. Because the loss of the intuitive grasp of things in their reasons by sense and intellect, sense must now be controlled firmly by the mind in order to minimize the damage done by the divorce between them (P. IV 855C–856B). Adam's "curse" (Gen. 3: 17–19) is a little more difficult to interpret, and Eriugena enlists the help of Maximus. According to that venerable father, the "earth" that is cursed is either Adam's own flesh or his heart: that which enjoys its brief pleasure, barren of virtue. The other reference to "earth" in Genesis 3:19 is understood to be the bliss of eternal life when the human body is dissolved back into the four elements from which it came (P. IV 858A–860A).

In this way Eriugena's exegesis, which begins with an account of the material obstacles, chiefly sexual division, which represent a fall from unity, focuses on the obstacles blocking the path of reason in the search for true knowledge of things in their causes. The constant struggle between sense and reason, derived ultimately from an exegesis of the Genesis text, is brought into a thoroughly Pauline context as Eriugena represents that struggle in terms of the conflict between the "inner and outer man." Perhaps the most important aspect to emerge from Eriugena's rearrangement of the events of the Genesis story is, as Otten puts it, that he "can decide for himself that man's inclination to evil is a *motus extra naturam* [movement outside nature], completely foreign to man's innate rationality."[10] As Eriugena says, "puffed up" mortal bodies come from sin and not from nature (P. II 571C–D).

Thus, Eriugena can, in a sense, counteract the negative effects of the fall by emphasizing the underlying rational character of human nature. Even though human nature fell from grace, its rationality is still able to function as a means of controlling the more base instincts of sense. As I have shown, Eriugena has used the Genesis text as the springboard for his understanding of human nature as divided and confused in an alien world. In this sense, we could say that his exegesis of a familiar text has taken him on a rather long journey through the complexities of the constitution of human nature.

The Promise of Paradise

I have already noted the positive way Eriugena views human nature; nowhere is this more evident than in his interpretation of paradise. Like Augustine before him, he notes that paradise is neither wholly corporeal nor wholly spiritual, although he does say, commenting on Ambrose, that paradise is "a spiritual garden sown with the seeds of the virtues and planted in human nature" (P. IV 841B). Eriugena's first conclusion regarding the nature of paradise is that it refers to the life human nature would have known had it remained obedient (P. IV 809B). However, because paradise has no past reality to sustain it, because human nature was not in paradise for any length of time (it fell as soon as it was created), Eriugena shifts his focus from past to future where paradise becomes an eschatological hope.[11] In this sense we can say that history's end and not its beginning becomes the focus of Eriugena's exegesis of the Genesis text. As his commentary progresses, Eriugena gives a much more definite meaning to paradise, which is nothing else than human nature in its divine aspect, as it was originally and as it will be.[12] This shifting of the experience of paradise from past to future constitutes a most radical move on Eriugena's part. According to Stock, Eriugena's paradise "has not altogether lost its historical reality . . . but that fragrant garden of Augustine is becoming so ethereal that Adam might not recognise it, were he given a second chance."[13] How does Eriugena argue to such a radical interpretation of a traditional story?

His exegesis of the Genesis text (2:9), constitutes a lengthy commentary on the meaning of the two trees of paradise: the tree of life (the "all-tree") and the tree of the knowledge of good and evil.[14] In this discussion, in which the Irish exegete follows Gregory of Nyssa and Ambrose of Milan closely, he concludes that paradise is human nature made in the image of God (P. IV 822A, 829C). The all-tree of paradise is the Word planted in the interior sense of human nature, which creates it, sustains it, indeed becomes it (P. IV 823B–824A, 825D–826C). The fruit of this tree is eternal life. The other tree, the tree of the knowledge of good and evil, is evil disguised as good and is planted in the exterior (corporeal) sense of human nature. The fruit of this tree is a mingled knowledge of good and evil, that is, a confused search after material things that satisfy carnal lusts (P. IV 827A). But who planted this tree in human nature? If God did, then God is responsible for evil. Eriugena's answer is that the form by which the tree seduces appears to be good and is from God, but the reaction to the tree is evil and cannot be from God (P. IV 827D–828A). The illustration used to demonstrate this point is the example of two people, one wise and the other greedy, both of whom see a beautiful vase of gold decorated with precious jewels. The wise person refers the beauty of the vase to its creator, while the greedy one is consumed with lust. For both of them the sensual image of the vase is beautiful, but they have different reactions to it: in the greedy person, lust comes from perverse will (P. IV 828B–829B). The fact that Eriugena locates this tree in the corporeal sense means that he can avoid the conclusion that evil exists substantially in human nature (P. IV 826B–827A). There is no evil in human nature itself, but evil can come from the "perverse and irrational motion of the free and rational will" (P. IV 828D). In this way Eriugena consolidates his thesis that the fall is a nonnatural movement (P. IV 828D), because in its substantial essence, human nature is perfect as it resides in the Word. In its embodiment, to those with eyes to see, "the beauty of the visible creature is referred to the glory of God" (P. IV 851A).

In identifying paradise with human nature and denying that human nature experienced paradise because of immediately turning away from God, Eriugena means that when the physical body is removed, the spiritual body will be as it was intended to be. Paradise, as something human nature is still waiting to experience, reveals that human nature's hidden dignity remains untouched and lies dormant until the final deification takes place. The simple, incorruptible, and heavenly body of humanity still lies hidden in the "secret place of nature" until that time when it will become the postresurrection body (P. IV 760A–B).[15] By transposing the elements of a familiar story, Eriugena not only provides a different focus for the story but also injects a strong element of optimism into the events surrounding the fall. Instead of lamenting about human misery, we find Eriugena confidently anticipating a future blissful state.[16] The end, according to Eriugena, is something new; it is not really a return to the scene of transgression since human nature was never really there at all. In chapter 7 I discuss further how Eriugena sees the return of human nature promised in Genesis.

As I have shown, the struggle of reason to come to the knowledge of things in their essences, that is, in their causes, is severely hampered because of the simultaneous knowledge and ignorance human nature has of itself. Given the fact that the concept of all sensible and intelligible things resides in the human mind, it would appear that the damaged intellect will have to overcome enormous obstacles in order to recover this knowledge. According to Otten, "all of creation is bound to disappear completely into the human mind . . . this man-centred view puts creation's existence severely at risk, for because of man's sin the attainment of true knowledge has as yet remained hidden from him."[17]

However, the resolution to this epistemic crisis is to be found in the humanity of the Word since it is in the Word that the perfection of human nature is to be found (P. IV 777B–C). In the Word, human nature can be seen in its pristine state.[18] Human nature is redeemed because of the Word who became fully human and yet remained untainted in order to heal the wound of perverted human nature (P. IV 777B–C). Relying heavily on Maximus the Confessor, Eriugena argues that the unification of human nature is achieved in Christ who restores all, both body and soul, for the Word does not return to the father alone but brings the whole of human nature back to the father (P. II 535D–539D, 571C–572A; IV 748A–C). Through the redemption of human nature which is effected in Christ, all of natura is unified and redeemed.[19] That Christ as the light of the world dispels the darkness of ignorance is a theme that Eriugena elaborates more fully in the *Homily on the Prologue of John* and in the poem *Aulae sidereae*, but it is not a prominent theme in the *Periphyseon*. There he concentrates on the more cosmic, redemptive role of the Word in the unification of human nature, which was humiliated in the "first man" and is exalted in the second, through which it can attain angelic status (P. II 575C).[20] Because of the fall, when "the unity of human nature was dissipated into infinite divisions and variations, the divine clemency ordained that there should be born a new Man in the world . . . in whom that nature which in the old man was divided should be called to its pristine unity" (P. II 563C–D).

Eriugena's fundamental assertion that the inclination to evil is not natural in human nature means that the senses do not impede fully the functioning of human rationality. Because of the Word planted in the interior sense, human nature is not severed completely from its divine origins: "the desire for the bliss which she had lost remained with her even after the Fall" (P. IV 777C–D; II 531C). The soul knows "through her intellect that from the one Cause of all things all things start upon their movement towards multiplicity without abandoning the simplicity of the unity by which they subsist in it eternally and immutably, and (move) towards it as the end of their whole movement, and end in it" (P. II 578D).

Despite the fall and the loss of the divine image, it could be argued that according to Eriugena's interpretation, the image of God within, the tree of the Word in the interior sense, still persists; that is precisely what gives him cause for optimism. In fact, just as the original creation was without the difference of sex, human nature is still without it, even in its embodied state, "to the extent that the image and likeness of the Creator exists in it" (P. II 541A). While human nature is in its actualized state, its intellect, which remains invisible, becomes manifest, comprehensible, apparent, visible, circumscribed, and embodied (P. III 633B–C). This text in the *Periphyseon,* which follows immediately upon the great theophanic text that expresses the manifestation of the unmanifest, not only ascribes to human nature that which is inherent in the creative capacity of the divine nature but firmly establishes the fact that human nature is capable of transcending its corporeal body in order to be reunited with its cause. Thus, because of this capacity, which is located in the intellect, human nature can ascend beyond itself to adhere to the creative nature, not through nature but through grace. "For in no created substance does there naturally exist the power to surpass the limits of its own nature and directly attain to the Very God in Himself" (P. II 576A–B). This power is granted through the Word, through the grace of the divine ray whereby human nature can once again discover God and itself.[21]

Thus, the hope of human nature as restored through the Word holds out hope for the whole of natura to be restored in human nature. In this sense, human nature becomes the turning point between procession and the reversion; just as all things were created in human nature, so too all things will begin the return journey through human nature (P. IV 723C).[22] But first human nature must overcome, with the assistance of the Word, its own splitting asunder in order to attain wholeness before the cosmic *reversio* can occur. This is effected through turning once again, or rather for the first time, toward the creator. In this sense we can understand the history of the world as summed up in the history of human nature.[23] Human nature, in its dignity as created in the image of God and in its capacity to redeem the whole of natura, which has been created in it, is "intimately connected with nature's dynamic core: *viz* its development."[24] This is the hope for which human nature strives and which it will attain in the final return of all things to that which neither creates nor is created.

Thus, at the heart of Eriugena's analysis of the human condition as a result of transgression lie hope and optimism. The dignity and honor of human nature is never forgotten, and it remains a fact that, despite sin, the glory of God shines forth from the divine image of the Word within it. "For God created the visible creature to this purpose, that through it, as likewise through the invisible, His glory might abound, and that He might be known . . . to be the One Creator of the whole creature, visible and invisible" (P. IV 843B). The liberties Eriugena takes in rearranging the events of the Genesis story, which is ultimately based on the fact that all creation occurred simultaneously, results in an attractive perspective on a much interpreted series of events.

PART III · THE WAY UP

THE RETURN

And the end of all our exploring
Will be to arrive where we started
And know the place for the first time.
                                        T. S. Eliot

The Resolution of Diversity

Reditus in Eriugena's thought is the means whereby the whole of creation, by an ineffable miracle, will be transformed into God. It signals the end of all division and opposition, constituting the very final scene in the great cosmic drama of the unfolding of division in the universe. The process of restoring to unity all complexity and diversity is the final great adventure of natura by which all things will be transposed from finitude to infinity so that God shall be "all in all." I have already shown that division operates on both an epistemological and on an ontological level in the *Periphyseon*. Every act of division can be resolved to unity; every outpouring is reciprocated by a converse movement. On a more differentiated level, God became human so that human might become God (*Hom.* XXI 295C) and in so doing effect the return of the whole of natura.

In its broad outline, the process of reditus appears to be extremely simple, although its interpretation and significance can at times be most complicated. It could be said that in the presentation of the return ("la théologie ascendante," as Cappuyns has described it) Eriugena's exegetical powers reached their summit.[1] The authorities Eriugena calls on to guide him in his explication of the journey back to the uncreated uncreating are Augustine, Ambrose,

Epiphanius, Gregory Nazianzus, Gregory of Nyssa, Maximus the Confessor, and the Pseudo-Dionysius; at times we find him maneuvering most skilfully to find his way amidst the various and sometimes contradictory positions. However, one should not ever be too quick to look for the source of all Eriugena's ideas. His understanding of the eschatological events awaiting humanity and indeed all creation is uniquely his own, although he is, at the same time, very anxious to find support in Eastern and Western patristic sources in relation to this most interesting topic.

Eriugena's speculations on the subject of reditus are by no means clearcut and well ordered. His speculations are found chiefly, though not exclusively, in book V of the *Periphyseon*, which, like book IV is extremely rich in scriptural texts and their exegesis. In dealing with the theme of return, we do well to remember that Eriugena's pronouncements on this subject are necessarily couched in terms of analogy and metaphor, devices employed by him, as the earlier fathers had employed them, to access or point to that which cannot be expressed literally. Given the difficulties in elucidating the process of exitus, it should come as no surprise that the process of reditus should also be characterized by complexity. The human mind, which uses illustrations from the things it can understand, cannot retranslate metaphor back into ordinary, literal terms. In forcing the mind beyond the literal meaning of any pronouncement through denial, the non-literal meaning can never be affirmed fully. The allegorical and metaphorical expressions used in *Periphyseon* V, which are always understood as traces or theophanies of the truth (P. II 614C), are typically patristic in their scriptural dependency and center on the great biblical themes of light, cloud, and darkness, topics I investigate further in the final section of this chapter.

Eschatological questions hold a certain fascination and attraction for all human beings, and Eriugena's speculations on the subject make interesting reading. Keeping in mind Eriugena's conception of the exitus as the self-manifestation of God in creation, which can be expressed in kataphatic terms, the reditus, as the complimentary movement, is, at least on one level, necessarily expressed in apophatic terms. The final turning of the circle back to the realm of the uncreated uncreating must be understood as movement from appearance and speech and knowledge to concealment, silence, and unknowing in the hidden darkness of the divine.

In book I of the *Periphyseon*, Eriugena asks a fundamental question: why should there be a return at all? The reasons why things must return to their source are elucidated as follows. He explains that, in very general terms, if things did not return to their source, they would remain worthless because the whole of creation is a manifestation of the image of God that must return to itself. "While by itself and in itself it is immutable and eternally at rest, yet it is said to move all things since all things through it and in it subsist and have been brought from not-being into being, for by its being, all things proceed out of nothing, and it draws all things to itself" (P. I 521C). Nature itself is cyclical in many aspects: in astronomical terms, the sun, moon, and stars, are all governed by the laws of cycle: they come forth at their appointed times and return.[2] Since all natural phenomena are governed by the laws of cycle, the whole of creation, which came forth from God, must return to God. Just as a magnet attracts iron without itself moving, so too the cause of all leads everything back to itself by the power of its beauty (P. I 520B). Eriugena also uses the examples of dialectic, arithmetic, geometry, music, and astronomy to illustrate that the beginning of all things is also their end (P. V 868D–869C).

In relation to the specific return of human nature which is the key to the return of all things, Eriugena begins in a most unlikely place, Genesis. According to his controversial exegesis, the return was promised when Adam and Eve were expelled from paradise (Gen. 3:22, P. V 861A–B). As Duclow explains, Eriugena's exegesis of this verse depends on a reading of the ambiguous particle *ne*, which can be read either negatively or interrogatively: "Now therefore let him not stretch forth his hand and take of the Tree of Life, eat and live forever" or "May he not perchance put forth his hand and take of the Tree of Life?"[3] Eriugena chose the interrogative interpretation in a spirit of obvious hope at a moment in human history when all seemed bleak. It is odd that Eriugena should have chosen this verse in the first place, for many other biblical texts could have served his purpose better and caused him fewer exegetical difficulties. However, it is in line with his general exegesis of the Genesis story that the promise of paradise should be given at the beginning of creation, and despite the difficulties involved in the exegesis of the Genesis text, Eriugena argues for the general return of all things to their source through human nature, which gains the image it had lost through the fall (P. IV 744B).

The unity that will result when God will be "all in all" is described by the familiar analogy derived from Maximus the Confessor: the presence of light in air. In the light of the sun, air appears to be nothing but light; so in the presence of God, human nature appears to be nothing but God (P. I 451B). Eriugena also uses the analogy of iron that is smelted in fire and becomes liquid; it is by reason alone that it is known as iron even though it is in a different form (P. I 451B). These analogies, which are repeated in book V (879A–B), are helpful in the broad sense toward an understanding of unity that still admits of distinction, for in the return, there is both destruction (because all things are, in fact, being changed) and preservation because they retain something of themselves in the ascent (P. V 876B, 893D)—an idea Eriugena had found in both Ambrose and Maximus. "So the sound intellect must hold that after the end of this world every nature, whether corporeal or incorporeal, will seem to be only God, while preserving the integrity of its nature, so that even God, Who in Himself is incomprehensible, is after a certain mode comprehended in the creature, while the creature itself by an ineffable miracle is changed into God" (P. I 451B).

In order to explain the simultaneous process of destruction and preservation in the return, Eriugena once again has recourse to a Neoplatonic analogy, this time to the Dionysian evocation of the unity perceived in the visual and auditory realms. Just as many voices make up one choir and many candles make up one light, so too, the many parts of creation can be said to make up one creation in God (P. V 883B–D). Eriugena also uses the example of a golden ball set upon the highest pinnacle of a tower: everyone can see it at the same time, and one person's vision does not obstruct the vision of another (P. V 883A–B). Therefore, while all things will be restored to their principle, each retains individual properties. In this sense, it becomes clear that Eriugena does not "conflate" God and creation, even in the final movement toward unity. In fact, the eradication and resolution of all distinction cannot take place on the ontological level as it can perhaps on the epistemological level. As I have shown, in the procession from God, God became not God yet remained God; in the return, the creature becomes not creature yet remains creature. God can be seen in the creature, and the creature, which is no longer called by the name of creature, can be seen in God (P. III 689A). The changing of human nature into God is not, therefore, a perishing of substance but is rather a return to the condition it would have enjoyed but lost through transgression (P. V 876B). It is not surprising that Eriugena held the view that individual substances do not perish in resolution because in the first instance, they were gift given and covered with grace. Second, he would have been most anxious to preserve the meaning of creation as the image and manifestation of God. Third, he wanted to "reconcile" his Neoplatonic and Christian sources on this point, for the concept of unity without loss of identity is a specifically Christian adaptation of a Neoplatonic theme. Creation cannot perish or become absorbed in the divine nature, rather, it returns to its primal pristine state. Some things in human nature, however, are mutable and do perish with the death of the body, but others endure and cannot be destroyed (P. V 872B). What is created in human nature according to nature will remain intact; what is added as a result of the fall will perish (P. IV 760C). The end of this life signals, as Maximus the Confessor had taught, not death but a separation from death (P. V 875D). Even though Eriugena is painstakingly fastidious in his explanation of the minutiae of the return process, we should perhaps be cautioned by his own words: "just as it passes all intellect how the word of God descends into man so it passes all reason how man ascends into God" (P. I 576C).

In the *Periphyseon,* the return, understood in terms of human nature, is the corollary movement of the fall from paradise and from angelic status (P. I 575A–C; V 949A). What is promised in the return is a sharing in the same status as the celestial essences (the angels), when all corporeality, sexuality, corruption, and modes of generation have been returned to their causes (P. II 575A). Every substance shall be purged of corruptible accidents and freed from the things that do not pertain to the state of their proper nature (P. III

666A). In the movement back to unity, in retracing the steps of divisoria into multiplicity, all of humanity shall be returned to its celestial source, but some human beings become more "angelized" than others (P. V 1020B).

The pivotal point in Eriugena's understanding of return is the incarnation of the Word. The Word descended in order to redeem the effects of those causes that are present in the Word and that are called back to the Word.[4] Eriugena's conception of the unification of all things is broadly christological in character: the "common end of the whole creation is the Word of God" (P. V 893A). The Word bears the responsibility for the salvation of all in calling all things back to their former state. "It was to bring human nature back . . . that the Incarnate Word of God descended, taking it upon Himself after it had fallen in order that He might recall it to its former state, healing the wounds of transgressions, sweeping away the shadows of false phantasies" (P. III 684A). The transformation of human nature into God is effected through the Word, who, in assuming human nature, raised it up (P. V 910D–911D). In book V of the *Periphyseon*, the nutritor and the alumnus engage in an interesting discussion regarding the resurrection of all sensible things in the Word (906C–908B). According to the nutritor, in assuming human nature, the Word assumed every creature made in that nature; therefore, all creation will be called back to its source through the Word (V 895B, 912B–C). Not only did the Word "exalt and bring back the humanity which He had received and refashioned in Himself to a parity with the angelic nature . . . but also exalted it above all angels and heavenly powers . . . above all things that are and all things that are not" (P. V 895B). Of course the alumnus asks the obvious question: will trees, plants, and animals also be restored in the Word? The answer of the nutritor is that all sensible things will return through human nature into their causes in which they exist substantially (V 914C–915A). Because all things were created in human nature, they cannot return except with it. According to Eriugena, who relies on Maximus at this point, human nature becomes the locus for the restoration of all created nature: "when man is recalled into the original grace of his nature, which he abandoned by transgression, he will gather again to himself every sensible creature below him through the wonderful might exercised by the Divine Power in restoring man" (P. II 534C). Interestingly, the question of animal soul is raised by the alumnus in *Periphyseon* book IV: do the souls of animals die with their bodies? The answer, which would most certainly endear Eriugena to some animal rights theorists today, is that any soul is superior to every body (736C–739C). This means that all souls will participate in and become one with the one primordial soul or life. This unification of natures means that all created nature becomes one nature, with a knowledge of the reasons of all things that are, equal to the knowledge of the angels (P. I 535A). Eriugena's account of the role of the incarnation of the Word as the starting point of the return is instrumental in that it signals the redemption of the fallen (P. V 910D–911B). Here we see, once again, Eriugena's reliance on the Pseudo-Dionysius, who viewed the redemptive role of the Word in a similar fashion. This is an interesting point in relation to Eriugena's reading of the great Eastern fathers, especially Maximus the Confessor. According to Eric Perl, the Eriugenian conception of the role of the Word, and his departure from the Eastern fathers in this respect, is most likely due to the fact that Eriugena was not greatly concerned with the technicalities of Byzantine Christology and its ontological significance. "For Maximus, the idea of incarnation, of hypostatic union, is the key to understanding the ontology of this relation. In Eriugena's system, on the other hand, it is possible to understand the metaphysical nature of creation and deification without reference to specifically christological doctrines. The fact of the incarnation is therefore additional, not intrinsic, to his ontology."[5]

Despite the rather inchoate Christology in Eriugena's works, the theme of drawing or calling in relation to the redemptive process effected through the Word shows Eriugena at his most poetic, and one is reminded very forcefully of the Plotinian description of the One calling all things back to itself through love (*Enn.* VI 7, 25, 2–6). The ascent is described by Eriugena on a number of occasions (betraying the influence of the Dionysian conception of *eros*) as a movement of love (P. I 519D–520A). Because God is loveable, God's beauty draws all things upward back to their source (P. III 680C): "He is the Cause of all love and is diffused through all things and gathers all things together into one and involves them in Himself in an ineffable Return, and brings to an end in Himself the motions of love of the whole creature" (P. I 519D–520A). However, although Eriugena often uses language reminiscent of the Neoplatonists, for the most part his discussion is concerned with the more technical aspects and details of eschatological events. The whole process of division, which had reached its completion with the creation of human beings (the crown and perfection of the six days work of creation), is the location for the start of the return through the Word (P. I 531D).

The General Return: Sinners and Saints

> For God shall be all in all, and every creature shall be
> overshadowed, that is, converted to God, as the stars when
> the sun arises. (P. III 689A)

There are numerous accounts of the return in the *Periphyseon,* one of which describes the "general return" of sensible creation and takes place in five stages (P. V 876A–B). The body is dissolved back into the four elements of the world; at the resurrection each will receive its own body back from the elements; the return of the body into spirit; the return of the spirit into the primordial causes; the whole of nature with the causes returns into God; then there will be only God. Another account of return retraces the process of division back to unity (P. V 893B–D). First, created nature is divided from what is not created; created nature is divided into sensible and intelligible; the sensible is divided into heaven and earth; paradise is distinguished from the inhabited globe; and humanity is segregated into male and female. The resolution of this articulation of divisoria (which is seen in Christ) begins when male and female have become unified as one humanity just as they were intended to be before the fall. Then, the inhabited globe is transformed into paradise; earthly bodies become heavenly bodies; the sensible creature is unified and transformed into intelligible creature; and the universal creature is united with its creator. Eriugena devotes a considerable amount of time to a discussion of why there will be no sexual difference in the resurrection (P. V 894A–895C; Gal. 3:28). Since sexual division was the result of turning away from the wholeness of its primal creation, to be rid of all division means that sexual division must also be transcended in unity through the Word. A third account of the return is more specific, and the seven stages outlined explain the specific return of human nature (P. V 1020C–D). Earthly body is changed into vital motion; vital motion into sense; sense into reason; and reason into mind. These four steps become one as all the sensible aspects of human nature are absorbed into reason, a step that takes place within nature. The final three steps go beyond nature: mind is absorbed into knowledge (knowledge of all things after God); knowledge into wisdom (which is knowledge of the truth); wisdom is transformed into the divine darkness, which is a "supernatural falling" into God himself (P. V 1021A).

One of the most interesting aspects of Eriugena's thought in relation to the return is that he is not elitist about who will make the return within human nature, for all created things must return to their source: sinners and saints alike shall be converted into spirit (P. V 948A); a celestial, angelic body will be restored to the just and the unjust after the resurrection (P. IV 764A). This theme is given a considerable amount of discussion in *Periphyseon* book V, and throughout the discussion the alumnus is extremely anxious to clarify the nature of punishment for the wicked. He is concerned chiefly with the consequences of asserting that the wicked will be damned eternally: "if the Word of God took human nature upon Him, it was not part of it . . . but the whole of it universally . . . then clearly, it is the whole of it which is restored in Him"(P. V 923C). But what about sinners and evil ones? Does this mean that hell does not exist? The dilemma is clearly stated: "either to eliminate the eternal punishment of wicked angels and men; or remove from a part of creation the dominion of the divine Goodness" (P. V 924C). The answer of the nutritor, in typical Neoplatonic fashion, depends on an understanding of evil as a privation of the good. Evil and sin, as alien to the divine nature, were not created by God (P. IV 826A, 827D–828A). "Whatever is not found in nature can by no means be found in the divine knowledge" (P. V 926A). The manner of sexual propagation, bodily increase and decrease, diseases, death, and the irrational impulses of the soul derive from matter; they originate from sin and are not, therefore, part of the primal creation. Accordingly, only these things will perish when creation will have become free from passions (P. I 511B; IV 763B; V 939D–940A).

The alumnus is only partially satisfied with the nutritor's response thus far, and he still wants to ascertain how the wicked will be punished. According to Eriugena's conception, since sin pertains to the will and not to nature, the nature even of wicked people cannot be punished. It is the will of wicked people and angels that shall abide in the torment of "empty dreams" for eternity (P. V 944A–945A). "Phantasies of evil" can never be destroyed and will be preserved in the consciences of evil-doers, who will be submerged eternally in profound ignorance of the truth (P. V 945B, 948C–D). The wicked will be denied a theophany of God; their "phantasies" will be cruel and will reflect their former vices (P. V 989A). Thus, according to Eriugena, God does not punish the wicked; their own consciences do that for them. This conclusion is consistent with Eriugena's exegesis of Genesis 3:14–19: God does not curse the things God has made (P. IV 848V). In the "shrine of wisdom" which is Christ, the distance between the blessed and the wicked is not spatial but is a distance that stems from merit. All must share in the same nature, but not all will share in the same grace.

All human bodies will be restored to unity and eternal immortality, but not all will be restored to bliss (P. II 584C–D). Only those "angels who are aflame with love of their creator" and only those people "who are called according to (the divine) purpose" will become deified (P. V 904A–B). This dual conception of return echoes the dual nature of the bestowal of gift and grace, of being and well-being, derived, as I have already noted, from James 1:17. All nature will return to its original state since all have been bestowed with the gift of being, which can never be taken away, but the grace of well-being involves the reward of deification, the exaltation of special souls, the blessed or elect. The divine goodness bestows not only being and well-being but also eternal being (P. V 903C–904A). Deification, being made God, is not, therefore, by nature but by grace (P. II 598C; III 666A; V 904D–905A).

> Not that even now God is not all in all, but after the sin of human nature and its expulsion from the abode of paradise, when, that is, it was thrust down from the height of the spiritual life and knowledge of the most clear wisdom into the deepest darkness of ignorance, no one unless illuminated by Divine Grace and rapt with Paul into the height of the Divine Mysteries can see with the sight of true understanding how God is all in all." (P. III 683C)

Holy souls are not only called back to paradise but, symbolically, are also called to eat of the tree of life itself.[6] Those who have gone beyond human nature in their holiness will not only be granted a "theophany" of God but will actually enter into the cloud of darkness surrounding God, to experience what Eriugena describes as a "theophany of theophanies" (P. I 450B; V 905C, 963C–964A, and 1020C).

The return of saints and sinners is illustrated by Eriugena using a scriptural illustration: the parable of the wise and foolish virgins.[7] The wise virgins represent the elect, who will be granted the highest theophany, while the foolish virgins represent those who will receive only a theophany. The lamps of the virgins represent their capacity for knowing the Light; only the wise, those who have overcome flesh and matter, will enter into the presence of God (P. V 1015B). Therefore, while all of human nature will be called to return to its original angelic status into paradise, the good will be called further: into God himself. For saints, as Eriugena explains, the many mansions in the Father's house signify the theophany of each of the elect (P. I 448C). That means that each will "see" God according to capacity, for one's place in the hierarchy of theophanies depends on one's conduct in this life (P. V 982C, 945C, 983A–984B). The Word gives a place to each and each receives according to their degree of sanctity and wisdom. Theophany is granted through grace in both the angelic and human natures "as a consequence of the descent of the Divine Wisdom and of the ascent of the human and angelic understanding" (P. I 449D). As far as the human intellect ascends through charity, the divine wisdom descends through compassion (P. I 449C).

Eriugena uses another very potent analogy for the theophany of the returned soul, interestingly an image used also by Plotinus. In the entry into the secret temple, each person is allotted a place according to merit and capacity: some are in outer porticos and some are further in and finally there are those who enter into the "shrine of wisdom" itself, which is the Word (P. V 905B–C, 926C–D, 945C–D, 983A). There, the elect will finally achieve the state they had lost: they will behold all things in their causes in the darkness that is, in fact, light. In the seventh and final stage of the return of the blessed, the deified enter into God himself, into the darkness of "inaccessible light" (1 Tim. 6:16), which shall then shine as day. It is in relation to the general and special returns in the *Periphyseon* that the story of Genesis is finally concluded. The "rest" of God on the sabbath day of Genesis is postponed until that general sabbath when all natura has reverted to its cause. Eriugena complements the sabbath of Genesis by adding a "sabbath of sabbaths" that signifies the return of the elect into God so that the "House of God shall be filled" (P. V 1016A).

Vision, Cloud, and Mystical Union

The concept of deification (*theosis*) of the elect is an idea Eriugena appropriated from Eastern sources; it was not, as he himself notes, a prominent idea in the thought of the theologians of the Latin West, with the exception of Ambrose: "weak eyes cannot bear the brilliance of the light" (P. V 1015C). Deification and the corresponding "vision" of God are also the focus for a most fruitful discussion of Eriugena's basic allegiance: Greek or Latin, Dionysian or Augustinian? I will argue here that Eriugena's conception of the final vision of God cannot easily be categorized as either Eastern or Western. While he does make a heroic effort to bring Augustine's ideas into line with what he had read in the Greek fathers, his conclusions are not fully dependent on either. The basic problem for Eriugena was to reconcile Augustine's conception of the vision of God with the Dionysian assertion that God can never be known or seen, even in the ultimate eschatological reunification of all things, a discussion that takes place very early in book I (P. 447A–448D). Although Eriugena found himself more at home with the fathers of the Greek church in stressing the idea of the absolute invisibility and unknowability of God, he was forced to hone his diplomatic skills to the utmost in confronting this apparently simple yet theologically vexing problem. How then does he resolve the two conflicting traditions?

Just as creation and the manifestation of God are more appropriately expressed in kataphatic terms, the converse movement of the resolution of division and multiplicity is understood best in apophatic terms. However, the difficulty of expressing the process of reditus in apophatic terms is obvious, and Eriugena's account relies heavily on parables and analogies that more appropriately express the return to the dark hiddenness of God, the uncreated uncreating. A conception of the final vision of God can appropriately be couched in terms of sight and vision, as Augustine had done, or in terms of blindness and darkness, as the Pseudo-Dionysius had done. However, with regard to the familiar Dionysian use of the dark symbolism, I will show that Eriugena differs from his most important Greek source in his attempt to unite Latin West with Greek East.

According to Eriugena's conception of the cosmic drama of salvation and redemption, light can be said to symbolize the procession of the light of the father, in the Word, who illumines the hidden places of darkness and ignorance.[8] The light metaphor, therefore, is used as an expression for the diffusion of all things from their causes into created effects. Eriugena's exegesis of the *fiat lux* of Genesis as the creation of the primordial causes signifies the transition from darkness to light, from the unknown to the known (P. III 691B–C; IV 781A–C). The positive connotations of Eriugena's use of the light metaphor can be said to involve a parallel understanding of the term "darkness" as symbolic of the fallen state of human beings: ignorance, damnation, evil, sin, hell, and privation, although he does refer to the transcendence of God as darkness and the vision of God via cloud (*Comm.* I xxv, 302B). In applying the terms "darkness" and "ignorance" both to God and to the human condition, Eriugena is using superlative and privative conceptions of darkness. I have explained elsewhere that the understanding of God as light belongs to a secondary account of theological analysis in the *Periphyseon*.[9] The movement of humanity from the light of paradise to the darkness of damnation after the fall and its complementary movement, through the light of the Word to the ineffable light of the divine nature is, I believe, situated within the overall, more general understanding of the process of creation from the original dark hiddenness of God into the light of manifestation and back once again to the concealment of darkness.

Eriugena's comments on the eschatological vision of human nature can be understood within this broad understanding. Although the vision promised in the life to come is the vision of God "face to face," Eriugena argues quite consistently that because God is invisible, the essence of God cannot be seen (P. I 448C). "Vision," therefore, must be mediated through theophany even for the elect (P. I 450C; V 926C, 988C). No creature, except the human nature of the Word, can ascend to God without any intervening theophany, although some theophanies ("theophanies of theophanies") are very close to God (P. V 905C). During the discussion of the beatific vision in *Periphyseon* book I, the alumnus asks whether this idea of mediated vision can "stand together" with the ideas of Augustine (P. I 450–C).[10] Eriugena's interpretation of Augustine's comments in the *City of God:*—"[t]hrough the bodies that we shall (have) put on, in every body we see wherever we turn the eyes of our body, we shall contemplate with translucent clarity God Himself" (XXII 29)—means that it is "through bodies in bodies" that we shall contemplate God, that is, through theophany or mediated vision. In this way Eriugena resolves for himself the conflict between Augustine and the Pseudo-Dionysius. Theophany, which Eriugena interprets as the "cloud of contemplation" (P. V 905C), is "vision" that is mediated because of God's invisibility and is, therefore, what is meant by vision "face to face" (P. I 448C; *Comm.* I xxv 302A–B). Therefore, Eriugena is consistent in maintaining the objective reference of divine incomprehensibility, even when God shall be "all in all." Indeed, in this respect Eriugena appropriates Gregory of Nyssa's interpretation of Philippians 3:13 (Paul's description of striving toward that which is ahead) in eschatological terms.[11] According to Eriugena, even in the return of all diversity to the unity of God, the quest for God will be endless, for although God is "found" in theophany to a certain extent, God is not found as to what God is in God's self (P. V 919A–D). "But since that which it seeks and towards which it tends . . . is infinite and not to be comprehended by any creature, it necessarily follows that its quest is infinite. . . . And yet although its search is unending, by some miraculous means it finds what it is seeking for: and again it does not find it, for It cannot be found" (P. V 919C). Therefore, even the highest of all theophanies will find only that God is, not what God is (P. V 1010C–D). This kind of knowledge would appear to be the limit of both the human and angelic orders, whether on earth or after the return to paradise.[12] The search for God will be infinite because the soul will always be beaten back by the radiance of the divine splendor. The unceasing and endless activity of the beatific life is simply seeking God.

In this respect, we can say that although Eriugena appears to favor the Eastern fathers, we can detect some ambiguity in his explanation of final theophany as "vision" of God. Although Eriugena would appear to have brought together some elements of Eastern and Western thought on the nature of eschatological events, to see the light/dark seeing/not-seeing theme as representative of a clear-cut division between East and West is too simplistic. The theological implications of either viewpoint have far-reaching consequences (at least on the speculative level) that transcend such primary differences. Eriugena would appear to have understood both traditions only too well, and it would seem that he has effected a worthy compromise between the two opinions. However, although the outward expression of his thought in relation to the nature of unity with God is more Augustinian than Dionysian, Eriugena's understanding of the final consequences of negative theology is no less radical than that of Dionysius and Gregory of Nyssa.

Although Eriugena is often thought of in the same terms as the Eastern fathers and the Pseudo-Dionysius with regard to the application and consequences of negative theology, his account of the final ontological resolution of the divisions of natura, does not, I believe, center on the experience (or lack of it) of the individual soul. In the *Mystical Theology* of the Pseudo-Dionysius, the "eyeless minds," through absolute ecstasy, enter into the cloud of divine darkness to a sightless and knowledgeless unity with the superessential once the sensible and intellectual have been abandoned fully. In the *Periphyseon,* an experience of unity with God developing out of sustained aphairetic practice on the part of the individual soul is not explicit. That is not to say that Eriugena was unaware of this theme in the thought of Gregory of Nyssa and the Pseudo-Dionysius. In *Periphyseon* book I he does mention the ascent of the individual soul to God in very Dionysian terms: "no one may draw near Him who does not first, by persevering in the way of thought, abandon all the senses and the operations of the intellect, together with the sensibles and everything that is and that is not, and, having achieved a state of not-knowing, is restored to the unity—as far as is possible—of Him who is above every essence and understanding" (P. I 510C; *Mystical Theology* I 1). The same Dionysian text is used in the *Homily on the Prologue of John*, where Eriugena speaks of the evangelist leaving behind reason and understanding and being raised unknowingly by wisdom and keenness of mind into those things that are beyond all things. Interestingly, in explaining how John was able to transcend himself and reach the highest wisdom, Eriugena makes the following comment: "John was, therefore, not just a man, but more than a man, when he rose above himself and all things" (*Hom.* V 285D, IX 288A).[13] This echoing of the Dionysian prayer for Timothy, which is also mentioned in book IV in support of the transcendence of human nature (759C), is all the more striking because John the Evangelist can be understood to have taken the place of Moses in the ascent to that which is above all. John even takes precedence over Paul, who was simply rapt into the third heaven (*Hom.* IV 285C). One further transformation of the Dionysian context is that because of being raised unknowingly into God, John is enabled to proclaim the Word. In the *Mystical Theology*, the soul, which has thrown itself blindly into the darkness of God, is silent in unspeakable unity with God. In the last analysis, for Eriugena, the purest form of knowledge of the transcendent God is through theophany, which is itself difficult enough. "For it is for the very few, wholly detached from earthly thoughts and purged by virtue and knowledge, to know God in these visible creatures" (P. III 689C–D). Even though Eriugena does make reference to the attainment of unity by those who, even in this life, have conquered the world and have ascended into God (he mentions the most conspicuous example, St. Paul being rapt into the third heaven and knowing God above every intellect; P. III 683C; V 920A, 982A–B, 999A), he does not develop the idea in relation to the individual ascent. The ability of the creature to go beyond itself and be joined to its creator as John and Paul did, is significant in the sense that it demonstrates that all human nature has the capacity to transcend sense and reason and, with the assistance of grace, be raised into God (P. V 949A–B, 988C). The attainment of true knowledge of all things, when reason and sense shall be made whole, is possible in this life, although it is generally understood to take place after the return of all things to their source, when the soul "will no longer be in ignorance of anything which is established within; for she will be encompassed by the Divine Light and turned towards God in Whom she will enjoy the perspicuous vision of all things" (P. IV 769B–C). Those who are "bathed in the splendour of the Divine ray, take the path of right contemplation and seek themselves and their God" are those deified by the action of the Word (P. V 844C).

The journey of Moses up to the cloud-wreathed summit of Sinai, which had been the prototype of the mystical ascent of the soul for Gregory of Nyssa and the Pseudo-Dionysius, is not a theme Eriugena develops in its original context (P. V 999A; *Comm.* I xxv 302B). Eriugena's transformation of the Dionysian conception of the epistemological and ontological condition of the restored soul, while not decreasing the force of negative theology and its consequences, gives it a new perspective. The shift from Old to New Testament texts and role models transforms the negative theology of Moses into the negative theology of John and Paul, as Eriugena focuses not on the cloud of Sinai but on the clouds of the ascension and transfiguration of the New Testament, using Maximus and Ambrose as his guides (Dan. 7:13, Matt. 26:64, and 1 Thess. 4:17). Thus, Eriugena's interpretation of the symbolism of cloud, darkness, and unknowing in relation to final events sets him apart from the Dionysian tradition. The eschatological dimension of his discussion puts it at one remove from the more immediate spiritual and epistemological significance, which is predominant in the writings of the Pseudo-Dionysius. In the *Periphyseon*, clouds symbolize the only means of experiencing a theophany of the invisible God (P. V 905C). The ascent into the "cloud of contemplation" is described as the highest theophany, the vision of God "face to face," wherein each will see God according to capacity. Clouds, as the "theophanies of the righteous," are the final resting place of the soul, for the transcendence of the divine nature is totally inaccessible. Therefore, the final stage of the return of the elect is a return to "inaccessible light."[14] The access to the inaccessible is limited in the sense that God is known and seen by not being known or seen: the returned soul knows that God is, not what God is, even in the highest theophanies granted to the most holy (P. V 919C, 1010D). And yet, access to the inaccessible is permitted, for theophany itself is, in some measure, the apparition of the unapparent (P. III 633A; II 557B); the ineffable light is present to all intellectual eyes but it cannot be known as to what it is, only that it is.

While the image of the purified, blinded soul throwing itself relentlessly against the ray of the divine darkness in the *Mystical Theology* of the Pseudo-Dionysius is not an image Eriugena uses, he does note, following Maximus, that the human spirit can ascend to God through perfect "sightlessness" (P. II 534C–535A). Generally, however, for Eriugena, the darkness over the abyss of Genesis 1 takes precedence over the darkness of Sinai that had been the foundation of the ascent to God in darkness in the writings of Gregory of Nyssa and the Pseudo-Dionysius. In the *Mystical Theology*, the purified soul enters into unity with the superessential in darkness; in the *Periphyseon*, the restored soul enters into a much-populated heavenly court. Eriugena's terminology implies that the vision of God is obscured through the unworthiness of created natures: the Seraphim hide their faces before the brilliance of God's light. In the *Periphyseon*, we find Eriugena develop the theme of return to God in terms of the cosmic *adunatio:* the whole of nature is hastening upwards towards its *telos* (P. V 929A–C).[15] In this sense, Eriugena's thought is generally focused in a cosmic, eschatological direction: eternal beatitude, achieved after death or at the end of the world, heralds entry into the contemplation of the truth for the different classes of beings (P. V 926C, 978D). The familiar spiritual ascent, described in the traditional terms of purgation, illumination, and union, is not a theme to which Eriugena directs his attention, nor does he advert to the method of aphairesis as used by Plotinus, Gregory of Nyssa, and the Pseudo-Dionysius. Gregory's theme of cleansing and purifying the soul of all that has been added so that God can be seen in the mirror of the soul is absent in Eriugena's writings. Purification in Gregory's works is a continuous struggle; according to Eriugena, the image of God is restored only after the end of time, although there is a passage in *Periphyseon* book II where Eriugena describes how the trinity of divine goodness cleanses the soul so that it can reflect the triune image more brilliantly (579A).

Eriugena does not look for an alternative "way" to God for the individual soul through mystical union: the unknowable, remains forever unknowable, even in final theophany when the soul is constantly seeking its end. Because of Eriugena's initial "sanctification" of creation, there is no need for the soul to look for God because in a very real sense, the soul is God. Eriugena's dependence on the theme of "eternal discovery," meant that he did not need to envisage a "solution" to the problem of knowledge of or unity with God. Therefore, even though many exponents of the negative way seek an alternative path to the unknowable through mystical union, Eriugena did not. His journey to the transcendent results in diversity within unity. The eschatological direction of Eriugena's thought, derived ultimately from Maximus the Confessor, sees Eriugena transposing the key from the individual level to the eschatological level. In his uncompromising expression of divine incomprehensibility and its eschatological consequences, he is totally consistent in following through the basic assertions of divine invisibility and incomprehensibility to their ultimate conclusions. What we encounter in *Periphyseon* book V is an expert and, at times, ingenious presentation of a coherent and attractive account of eschatological events that found its inspiration in the momentous events of the Genesis story.

IN RETROSPECT

In this short epilogue I will not document the history of Eriugena's influence after his death; that has been done elsewhere.[1] Instead, I would like to offer a few general comments on some of the themes in Eriugena's works that I find particularly appealing. Although it is regrettable that the *Periphyseon* was subject to various condemnations, the interest in Eriugena today bears testimony not only to his "modern" approach to difficult philosophical and theological problems but also to the fact that those who seek the truth with a right spirit will attract others who share their vision.

Of the many themes in Eriugena's works that are especially significant for me, perhaps his astute and penetrating unraveling of natura is the most exciting. Despite his ingenious, and at times extremely complicated, approach to uncreated and created reality, Eriugena consistently points up the mystery that lies at the heart of all reality. As we reach the end of the century that has seen the most advanced scientific and technological inventions in human history, we are not much nearer an explanation of created natura. In fact, many of our attempts to master nature have had disastrous consequences in terms of the ruthless plunder of nature. The modern conception of the dichotomy conceived to exist between reason and nature sets human beings apart from nature and all other species. Eriugena's much more holistic and perspectival approach to the whole of created reality does not suppose a strict hierarchy (which inevitably leads to dominators and the dominated) but, rather, perceives all things as bound together in an ineffable harmony. Technological advances can result in our forgetfulness of nature and the fact that human nature is a part of it. The obvious reverence Eriugena had for nature—an attitude that is becoming increasingly more evident in contemporary environmental ethics—serves to remind us that even in our frenzy to technologize our lives and all that surrounds them, we human beings will ultimately return to the earth from which we came.

The contemporary scientific debate among physicists and biologists concerning the Gaia hypothesis of James Lovelock demonstrates that despite Stephen Weinburg's dreams of a "final theory" and Stephen Hawkings's audacious attempts to "read the mind of God," it remains as elusive as ever in that the universe does not give up its secrets easily. Its detailed and intricate harmony cannot be examined in the way we would examine the various parts of a symphonic score, but the whole can be grasped and partly if not fully understood. One is reminded of "God's Grandeur" by the Jesuit poet Gerard Manley Hopkins, who shared the same sense of reverence for nature:

> And for all this nature is never spent;
> There lives the dearest freshness deep down things . . .
> Because the Holy Ghost over the bent
> World broods with warm breast and with ah! bright wings.

Another aspect of the mystery at the heart of reality is that what is there is no rationality of being but instead the opacity of "nothing," which goes beyond all that human beings can know.[2] This mystery seems somehow appropriate in an age that is characterized by spiritual search but is also one that does not seek restrictive boundaries. Today, negative theology, and all that it entails, plays a considerable role in contemporary philosophical speculation (Jacques Derrida, Jean-Luc Marion, Jacques Lacan, and Theodor Adorno, among others). Whether we would go so far as Marion and claim that some forms of positive conceptualization and theorizing about God constitute idolatry is not certain.[3] Eriugena himself allowed that each one should "hold what opinion he will until that Light shall come which makes the light of the false philosophers a darkness and converts the darkness of those who truly know into light" (P. V 1022C).

While it is true that many followers of the negative way have, throughout history, been subject to condemnations and charges of heresy, it is also true that their vision has been unencumbered with the strict categories that mark many conceptions of God. Yet it must be said that Eriugena was a negative theologian with a difference. When one reads the *Mystical Theology* of the Pseudo-Dionysius or some of the vernacular sermons of Meister Eckhart, one often gets the impression that they want to "disrobe" God, to lay hold of God in God's nakedness, that is, to come to a mystical knowledge of God as God is in God's self. Eriugena's focus is slightly different: God can never be perceived in God's nakedness precisely because God is intimately involved in creation. The various divisions of universal *natura* include the uncreated as well as the created, and together they make up one mysterious whole. It is here perhaps that Eriugena differs most from the more obvious followers of the Neoplatonists. As Hans Urs Von Balthasar put it, Eriugena presents "the whole world-picture taken over from the philosophers and fashioned into a Christian utterance."[4]

One further theme that, I believe, could have tremendous appeal today is Eriugena's conception of being as gift that is received by all alike. Since the beginning is intimately bound up with the end in Eriugena's thought, this theme finds its ultimate logical conclusion in his conception of the final return of all things to their source. Precisely because being is a gift that is freely given, it can never be taken away, even from those who did not use their gift well. Eriugena's explanation of God's rebuke of Adam and Eve and his fundamental belief in the intrinsic goodness of human nature prefigures that which awaits human beings at the end of this present life. The common perception of hell and damnation and the punishments that await the unjust (admirably evoked by a more recent Irishman, James Joyce in *A Portrait of the Artist as a Young Man*) are strikingly absent in Eriugena's thought. In a fashion that is likely to be much more appealing today, Eriugena portrays the whole of creation returning to its source, not to receive punishment from an angry God, but to receive a theophany of God that reflects the kind of life lived. Thus, just as human nature is responsible for its own downfall, so too it is responsible for its own heavenly reward. Eriugena's egalitarian approach in terms of the return to paradise, which is a logical conclusion to the idea that human nature never really was there in the beginning, is a very modern approach to a much-discussed question.

In the preface I note that I do not intend to deal with Eriugena's more theological works (that would constitute a book in itself). However, after this examination of some Eriugenian themes, it should be made clear that Eriugena the philosopher cannot be separated from Eriugena the theologian. We cannot read the works of Eriugena from the modern viewpoint that philosophy and theology can be distinguished clearly. I believe that Eriugena's worldview, especially as he presents it in the *Periphyseon,* is, as Werner Beierwaltes put it, "the most compelling and internally coherent paradigm of philosophical or speculative theology in the early Middle Ages."[5]

The mark of Eriugena's genius is that his works are finally coming into their own after centuries of neglect and condemnation. Ireland, the land of saints and scholars—which can claim very few philosophers among its great and famous—is finally reclaiming one of its own with vigor and a great deal of pride.

NOTES

Preface

1. Epigram attributed to Eriugena, translated by Michael Herren in "Johannes Scottus Poeta," in *From Augustine to Eriugena: Essays on Neoplatonism and Christianity in Honor of John O'Meara*, ed. F. X. Martin and J. A. Richmond (Washington, D.C.: Catholic University of America Press, 1991), p. 97.

Chapter 1

1. D. Knowles, *The Evolution of Medieval Thought*, 2nd ed. (London: Longman, 1988), p. 69.

2. For example, Greek prayers were used both in the Aachen church and at the Abbey of St. Denis; see É. Jeauneau, "Jean Scot Érigène et le grec," *Archivium Latinitatis Medii Aevi* 41 (1979), pp. 5–50.

3. For various views on this question, see M. Cappuyns, *Jean Scot Érigène, sa vie, son oeuvre, sa pensée* (Louvain, Belgium: Mont César, 1933), pp. 234–5, and Michael Herren, "Eriugena's 'Aulae sidereae', the 'Codex Aureus' and St Mary's of Compiègne," *Studi Medievali*, series 3, 28 (1987), pp. 593–608.

4. J. J. Contreni, "Carolingian Biblical Culture," in *Iohannes Scottus Eriugena: The Bible and Hermeneutics*, ed. G. Van Riel, C. Steel, and J. J. McEvoy (Leuven, Belgium: Leuven University Press, 1996), p. 3.

5. A concise account of Christian education and the role of the liberal arts in the ninth century can be found in B. B. Price, *Medieval Thought: An Introduction* (Oxford: Blackwell, 1992), pp. 50–68.

6. *Jean Scot Érigène*, p. 26; see also the collected articles of L. Bieler, *Ireland and the Culture of Early Medieval Europe*, ed. R. Sharpe (Aldershot, Hampshire: Variorum Reprints, 1987).

7. See Cappuyns, *Jean Scot Érigène*, pp. 25–26.

8. See J. J. Contreni, "The Irish 'Colony' at Laon during the time of John Scottus," in *Jean Scot Érigène et l'histoire de la philosophie*, ed. R. Roques (Paris:

CNRS, 1977), pp. 59–68; see also the same author's collected papers: *Carolingian Learning, Masters and Manuscripts* (Aldershot, Hampshire: Variorum Reprints, 1992).

9. For a discussion of Eriugena's connection with the Irish hexaemeral tradition, see T. O'Loughlin, "Unexplored Irish Influence on Eriugena," *Recherches de Théologie ancienne et médiévale* 59 (1992), pp. 23–40; the edition of Eriugena's biblical glosses reveals his own native scholarly tradition in the use of Old Irish words; see J. J. Contreni and P. P. O Néill, *Glossae Divinae Historiae: The Biblical Glosses of John Scottus Eriugena*, Millennio Medievale 1 (Florence: Sismel Edizioni del Galluzzo, 1998).

10. See G. Madec, "L'augustinisme de Jean Scot dans le 'De praedestinatione,'" in Roques, *Jean Scot Érigène et l'histoire de la philosophie*, pp. 183–90; see also W. Otten's brief analysis of this treatise in "Eriugena's *Periphyseon*: A Carolingian Contribution to the Theological Tradition," in *Eriugena East and West*, ed. B. McGinn and W. Otten (Notre Dame, Indiana: University of Notre Dame Press, 1994), pp. 79–83; for a concise presentation of the theological background to the problem of predestination see J. Pelikan, *The Growth of Medieval Theology (600–1300). The Christian Tradition: A History of the Development of Doctrine* 3 (Chicago: University of Chicago Press, 1978), pp. 80–98.

11. Eriugena's text has been edited by G. Madec, *Iohannis Scotti De divina praedestinatione liber*, Corpus Christianorum, Continuatio Mediaevalis 50 (Turnhout, Belgium: Brepols, 1978), and translated by M. Brennan: John Scottus Eriugena, *Treatise on Divine Predestination*, Notre Dame Texts in Medieval Culture 5 (Notre Dame, Indiana: University of Notre Dame Press, 1998).

12. References to primary sources are generally given in the text hereafter, while other references and comments are found in the footnotes. All references to the *Periphyseon* (P) give the number of the book and the reference to the *Patrologia Latina* edition of H.-J. Floss, vol. 122 (Paris: 1853); this has been done in order to ensure uniformity, since book V has not yet appeared in critical edition. Quotations from the *Periphyseon* follow the version of I. P. Sheldon-Williams, revised by J. J. O'Meara, *Eriugena Periphyseon (The Division of Nature)*, Cahiers d'études médiévales, Cahier spécial 3 (Washington: Dumbarton Oaks, 1987).

13. *The Growth of Medieval Theology (600–1300)*, pp. 50–52.

Chapter 2

1. Henry Bett, *Johannes Scotus Erigena: A Study in Medieval Philosophy* (Cambridge: Cambridge University Press, 1925).

2. See, for example, Alice Gardner, *Studies in John the Scot (Erigena): A Philosopher of the Dark Ages* (London: Oxford University Press, 1900).

3. Mary Brennan's useful collection of materials for a biography of Eriugena should be consulted by those wishing to review the material first made available by Cappuyns in 1933, taking into account later scholarship; see M. Brennan, "Materials for the Biography of Johannes Scottus Eriugena," *Studi Medievali*, series 3, 28 (1986), pp. 413–60.

4. See M. Cappuyns, *Jean Scot Érigène, sa vie, son oeuvre, sa pensée* (Louvain, Belgium: Mont César, 1933), pp. 252–53.

5. Ibid., pp. 66–67.

6. Recent scholarship has stressed the importance of an understanding of Irish learning for the correct situation of Eriugena in his context; see G. V. Murphy, "The Place of John Eriugena in the Irish Learning Tradition," *Monastic Studies* 14 (1983), pp. 93–107, and T. O'Loughlin, "Unexplored Irish Influence on Eriugena," *Recherches de Théologie ancienne et médiévale* 59 (1992) pp. 23–40.

7. M. Cappuyns, *Jean Scot Érigène*, pp. 252–53.

8. Ibid., p. 255.

9. For the most recent edition of Eriugena's poetry with English translation, see M. Herren, *Iohannis Scoti Carmina*, Scriptores Latini Hiberniae, vol. 12 (Dublin: Dublin Institute for Advanced Studies, 1993).

10. C. E. Lutz, ed., *Iohannis Scotti Annotationes in Marcianum* (Cambridge, Mass.: Medieval Academy of America, 1939); É. Jeauneau, ed., "Le Commentaire érigénien sur Martianus Capella, De nuptiis Lib. I, d'après le manuscrit d'Oxford Bodl. Lib. Auct. T. 2. 19, fol. 1–31," *Quatre thèmes érigéniens* (Montréal: Institut d'Études Médiévales, 1978), pp. 101–86; see also M. Herren, "The Commentary on Martianus Attributed to John Scottus: Its Hiberno-Latin Background," in *Jean Scot écrivain*, ed. G.-H. Allard (Montréal: Bellarmin, 1986), pp. 265–86.

11. C. Laga and C. Steel, eds., *Maximi Confessoris, Quaestiones ad Thalassium I (Q. I-LV) una cum latina interpretatione Ioannis Scotti Eriugenae*, Corpus Christianorum, Series Graeca 7 (Turnhout, Belgium: Brepols, 1980); M. Cappuyns, ed., "Le 'De imagine' de Grégoire de Nysse traduit par Jean Scot Érigène," *Recherches de Théologie ancienne et médiévale* 32 (1965), pp. 205–62; É. Jeauneau, *Maximi Confessoris Ambigua ad Iohannem iuxta Iohannis Scotti Eriugeneae latinam interpretationem*, Corpus Christianorum, Series Graeca 18 (Turnhout, Belgium: Brepols, 1988).

12. A good introduction to the Pseudo-Dionysius can be found in A. Louth, *Denys the Areopagite*, Outstanding Christian Thinkers Series (London: Chapman, 1989). The works of the Pseudo-Dionysius have been translated into English by C. Luibheid and P. Rorem, *Dionysius the Areopagite: The Complete Works*, Classics of Western Spirituality Series (London: SPCK, 1987); on the Pseudo-Dionysius and Maximus the Confessor in relation to Eriugena, see J. J. O'Meara, *Eriugena* (Oxford: Oxford University Press, 1988), pp. 51–79.

13. The text of Eriugena's Dionysian translations is printed in *Dionysiaca*, ed. Ph. Chevallier, 2 vols. (Bruges: Desclée de Brouwer, 1937 and 1950).

14. For discussion of Eriugena's achievements as a translator from the Greek, see R. Roques, "Traduction ou interprétation? Brèves remarques sur Jean Scot traducteur de Denys," in *The Mind of Eriugena*, ed. J. J. O'Meara and L. Bieler (Dublin: Irish University Press, 1973); see also É. Jeauneau, "Jean Scot Érigène et le grec," *Archivium Latinitatis Medii Aevi* 41 (1979), pp. 5–50, and I. P. Sheldon-Williams, "Eriugena's Interpretation of the Pseudo-Dionysius," *Studia Patristica*, ed. E. Livingstone (Berlin: Akademie, 1975), p. 151.

15. The commentary has been edited by J. Barbet, *Iohannis Scoti Eriugenae: Expositiones in ierarchiam coelestem*, Corpus Christianorum, Continuatio Mediaevalis 31 (Turnhout, Belgium: Brepols, 1975).

16. J. McGinn, "The Originality of Eriugena's Spiritual Exegesis," in *Iohannes Scottus Eriugena. The Bible and Hermeneutics*, ed. G. Van Riel, C. Steel, and J. J. McEvoy (Leuven, Belgium: Leuven University Press, 1996), p. 72.

17. See "Biblical Contradictions in the *Periphyseon* and the Development of Eriugena's Method," in Van Riel, Steel, and McEvoy, *Iohannes Scottus Eriugena: The Bible and Hermeneutics*, especially pp. 117–9.

18. See Contreni, "Carolingian Biblical Culture," in Van Riel, Steel, and McEvoy, in *Iohannes Scottus Eriugena: The Bible and Hermeneutics*, p. 9.

19. A. Kijewska's excellent article on Eriugena's use of John the Evangelist brings out a perspective of Eriugena's thought that shows not only his augustinian inheritance but also his gift for originality; see "The Eriugenian Concept of Theology. John the Evangelist as the Model Theologian," in Van Riel, Steel, and McEvoy, *Iohannes Scottus Eriugena: The Bible and Hermeneutics*, pp. 173–93; É. Jeauneau has edited Eriugena's commentaries on John; see *Jean Scot: Homélie sur le Prologue de Jean*, Sources chrétiennes 151 (Paris: Éditions du Cerf, 1969), and *Jean Scot: Commentaire sur l'évangile de Jean*, Sources chrétiennes 180 (Paris: Éditions du Cerf, 1972); hereafter I abbreviate these works as *Hom.* and *Comm.*

20. A good collection of articles on Eriugena's sources can be found in *Eriugena: Studien zu seinen Quellen*, ed. W. Beierwaltes (Heidelberg: Carl Winter Universitätsverlag, 1980).

21. E. Gilson, *History of Christian Philosophy in the Middle Ages* (New York: Random House, 1955), p. 121.

22. See B. Stock, "In Search of Eriugena's Augustine," in Beierwaltes, *Eriugena: Studien zu seinen Quellen*, pp. 85–104; B. Stock, "Observations on the use of Augustine by Johannes Scottus Eriugena," *Harvard Theological Review* 60 (1967), pp. 213–20; J. J. O'Meara, "Eriugena's use of Augustine," *Augustinian Studies* 11 (1980), pp. 21–34, and, in relation to the hexaemeral commentaries, see T. O'Loughlin, "Unexplored Irish Influence on Eriugena," *Recherches de Théologie ancienne et médiévale* 59(1992), especially pp. 29–37.

23. See I. P. Sheldon-Williams, "The Greek Christian Platonist Tradition from the Cappadocians to Maximus and Eriugena," in *The Cambridge History of Later Greek and Early Medieval Philosophy*, ed. A. H. Armstrong (Cambridge: Cambridge University Press, 1967), pp. 521–33, and "Eriugena's Greek Sources," in O'Meara and Bieler, *The Mind of Eriugena*, p. 5; T. Tomasic has more recently evaluated Eriugena in the light of his Dionysian influence; see "The Logical Function of Metaphor and Oppositional Coincidence in the Pseudo-Dionysius and Johannes Scottus Eriugena," *Journal of Religion* 68 (1988), pp. 364–67; see also É. Jeauneau, "Pseudo-Dionysius, Gregory of Nyssa and Maximus the Confessor in the Works of John Scottus Eriugena," in *Carolingian Essays: Andrew Mellon Lectures in Early Christian Studies*, ed. U.-R. Blumenthal (Washington, D.C.: Catholic University of America Press, 1983), pp. 175–87.

24. Giulio d'Onofrio, "The Concordance of Augustine and Dionysius: Toward a Hermeneutic of the Disagreement of Patristic Sources in John the Scot's *Periphyseon*," in *Eriugena East and West*, ed. B. McGinn and W. Otten (Notre Dame, Indiana: University of Notre Dame Press, 1994), pp. 115–40.

25. "Eriugena's *Periphyseon:* A Carolingian Contribution to the Theological Tradition," in McGinn and Otten, *Eriugena East and West,* p. 73.

26. "Remarks on Eastern Patristic Thought in John Scottus Eriugena," in McGinn and Otten, *Eriugena East and West,* pp. 58–59.

27. In addition to completing the edition of the *Periphyseon* begun by Sheldon-Williams, Jeauneau has also embarked on a new and revolutionary edition of the *Periphyseon.* Because of the fact that it is extremely difficult to establish a definitive text, Jeauneau has printed various versions of the text side by side, showing the evolution of the text through different corrected versions (some of which were revised by Eriugena himself). As the editor points out in the introduction, a text is rather like a film, as opposed to something that has been made fast; see *Johannis Scotti seu Eriugenae, Periphyseon liber primus,* Corpus christianorum, Continuatio Mediaevalis 161 (Turnhout, Belgium: Brepols, 1996) *liber secundus,* CCM, 162 (Turnhout, Belgium: Brepols, 1997), and *liber tertius,* CCM, 163 (Turnhout, Belgium: Brepols, 1999).

28. See *Iohannis Scotti Eriugenae Periphyseon Liber Quartus,* Scriptores Latini Hiberniae, volume 13 (Dublin: Dublin Institute for Advanced Studies, 1995), pp. xii–xiii; for an excellent summary of the five books of the *Periphyseon,* see J. J. O'Meara, *Eriugena,* chaps. 5–8.

29. See the introduction to his edition of book IV of the *Periphyseon,* p. xi.

30. Otten, "Eriugena's *Periphyseon:* A Carolingian Contribution to the Theological Tradition," pp. 70–71.

Chapter 3

1. Proclus, *Elements of Theology* prop. 35; *Celestial Hierarchy* I 1, XV 1.

2. "The Uplifting Spirituality of Pseudo-Dionysius," in *Christian Spirituality: Origins to the Twelfth Century,* ed. B. McGinn, J. Meyendorff, and J. Leclercq, World Spirituality 16 (New York: Crossroad, 1988), p. 147.

3. See D. Moran, *The Philosophy of John Scottus Eriugena: A Study of Idealism in the Middle Ages* (Cambridge: Cambridge University Press, 1989), pp. 214–18, and G. Piemonte, "L'expression 'quae sunt et quae non sunt': Jean Scot Érigène et Marius Victorinus," in *Jean Scot écrivain,* ed. G.-H. Allard (Montréal: Bellarmin, 1986), pp. 81–113; on the modification of the Boethian and Dionysian understanding of all that is and all that is not, see D. J. O'Meara, "The Concept of *Natura* in John Scottus Eriugena (*De divisione naturae* Book I)," *Vivarium* 19:2 (1981), especially pp. 126–33.

4. See W. Otten, *The Anthropology of Johannes Scottus Eriugena,* Brill's Studies in Intellectual History 20 (Leiden: Brill, 1991), p. 4.

5. R. Roques, "Remarques sur la signification de Jean Scot Érigène," *Divinitas* 11 (1967), p. 270.

6. See D. Moran, *Philosophy,* pp. 250–51, and I. P. Sheldon-Williams, "The Greek Christian Platonist Tradition from the Cappadocians to Maximus and Eriugena," in *The Cambridge History of Later Greek and Early Medieval Philosophy,* ed. A. H. Armstrong (Cambridge: Cambridge University Press, 1967), pp. 521–23; Sheldon-Williams suggested that the fourth division of nature is derived from Pythagorean number theory, which Eriugena would have

known from Philo through Origen; on the relationship between Philo's division of numbers and Eriugena's division of nature; see É. Jeauneau, "Le thème du retour," in *Études érigéniennes* (Paris: Études augustiniennes, 1987), especially pp. 367–68.

7. *Anthropology*, p. 35.

8. On Eriugena's approach to the concept of natura as an open system that is approached by division rather than definition, see Otten, *Anthropology*, pp. 16–7, and "The Universe of Nature and the Universe of Man: Difference and Identity," in *Begriff und Metapher: Sprachform des Denkens bei Eriugena*, ed. W. Beierwaltes (Heidelberg: Carl Winter Universitätsverlag, 1990), especially pp. 202–5; see also O'Meara, "The Concept of *Natura* in John Scottus Eriugena," pp. 126–45.

9. Eriugena frequently uses the texts 1 Tim. 6:16 and Ps. 139:12 in support of the Dionysian idea that the darkness of God is truly light; see *Mystical Theology* I 1. H.-Ch. Puech's seminal article on divine darkness gives an excellent background to this theme; see "La ténèbre mystique chez le Pseudo-Denys et dans la tradition patristique," *Études carmélitaines* 23 (1938), pp. 33–53.

10. See "Eriugena's Use of the Symbolism of Light, Cloud, and Darkness in the *Periphyseon*," in *Eriugena East and West*, ed. B. McGinn and W. Otten (Notre Dame, Indiana: University of Notre Dame Press, 1994), pp. 141–52; on the themes of light and the manifestation of God and the metaphysics of light, see W. Beierwaltes, "*Negati Affirmatio*: Welt als Metapher," in *Jean Scot Érigène et l'histoire de la philosophie*, ed. R. Roques (Paris: CNRS, 1977), pp. 127–59, and J. J. McEvoy, "Metaphors of Light and Metaphysics of Light in Eriugena," in W. Beierwaltes, *Begriff und Metapher*, pp. 149–67.

11. In relation to the theocentric conception of reality, see E. Perl, "Metaphysics and Christology in Maximus the Confessor and Eriugena," in McGinn and Otten, *Eriugena East and West*, especially pp. 253–61.

12. Otten, *Anthropology*, p. 71.

13. On God's being as non-being or intellect in Eckhart's thought, see the *Parisian Questions and Prologues*, especially question 1.

14. The concepts non-being and beyond being in relation to the transcendence of God derive from Neoplatonic interpretations of some Platonic texts, primarily the *Republic* (509B) and *Parmenides* (142A); see the chapters on Plotinus and Proclus in D. Carabine, *The Unknown God: Negative Theology in the Platonic Tradition: Plato to Eriugena* (Louvain, Belgium: Peeters, 1995).

15. See D. Moran's explanation of this point in *Philosophy*, pp. 212–17.

16. See M. L. Colish, "Carolingian Debates over *Nihil* and *Tenebrae*: A Study in Theological Method," *Speculum* 59 (1984), pp. 757–95; see also E. Gilson, *History of Christian Philosophy in the Middle Ages*, pp. 111–12, and D. Moran, *Philosophy*, p. 11.

17. On the rather dubious origin of the inclusion of *materia* with God and the primordial causes, which is found in one manuscript only, see A. Wohlman, "L'ontologie du sensible dans la philosophie de Scot Érigène," *Revue Thomiste* 83 (1983), pp. 558–82; reprinted in A. Wohlman, *L'homme, le monde sensible et le péché dans la philosophie de Jean Scot Érigène* (Paris: Vrin, 1987), pp. 42–66.

18. See *Celestial Hierarchy* IV 1 and Gregory of Nyssa, *Against Eunomius* II 259–60, where Gregory argues that if we take accidents from a body (shape, weight, color, and so on), there is nothing left to perceive.

19. An interesting passage in Augustine's *Confessions* applies the same kind of reasoning to created reality: things are in so far as they are from God, but are not in so far as they are not God; see VII 11.

20. See *Philosophy*, p. 218.

21. Ibid.

22. *Anthropology*, p. 44.

23. The Pseudo-Augustinian *Categoriae decem*, a Latin summary of Aristotle's *Categories*, was an important source for Eriugena's development of the idea that the categories cannot be attributed to God. Eriugena's own commentary was also significant in terms of the development of later Medieval thought; see J. Marenbon, "John Scottus and the 'Categoriae Decem,'" in *Eriugena: Studien zu seinen Quellen*, ed. W. Beierwaltes (Heidelberg: Carl Winter Universitätsverlag, 1980), pp. 117–34.

24. Ibid., p. 120.

25. A useful elucidation of the category of ousia can be found in D. Moran, "Time, Space and Matter in the *Periphyseon:* An Examination of Eriugena's Understanding of the Physical World," in *At the Heart of the Real*, ed. F. O'Rourke (Dublin: Irish Academic Press, 1992), pp. 68–89.

Chapter 4

1. For general comments on this theme, see P. W. Rosemann, "A Change of Paradigm in the Study of Medieval Philosophy: From Rationalism to Postmodernism," *American Catholic Philosophical Quarterly* 72:1 (1998), p. 60.

2. W. Otten, *The Anthropology of Johannes Scottus Eriugena*, Brill's Studies in Intellectual History 20 (Leiden: Brill, 1991), p. 36.

3. "Divine Nothingness and Self-Creation in John Scottus Eriugena," *Journal of Religion* 57 (1977), pp. 114–15; see also É. Jeauneau, "Néant divin et théophanie: Érigène disciple de Denys," *Diotima* 23 (1995), pp. 121–27.

4. *Mystical Languages of Unsaying* (Chicago: University of Chicago Press, 1994), p. 59.

5. See E. Perl's comments on this theme in "Metaphysics and Christology in Maximus the Confessor and Eriugena," in *Eriugena East and West*, ed. B. McGinn and W. Otten (Notre Dame, Indiana: University of Notre Dame Press, 1994), especially pp. 253–57; according to Dermot Moran's thesis, Eriugena's meontology represents a deconstruction of the hierarchical ontology of the Neoplatonists because the four divisions of nature are to be understood perspectively as theophany, as the manifestation of one ontological order; see *The Philosophy of John Scottus Eriugena: A Study of Idealism in the Middle Ages* (Cambridge: Cambridge University Press, 1989) pp. 99–102 and 254.

6. "Remarks on Eastern Patristic Thought in John Scottus Eriugena," in McGinn and Otten, *Eriugena East and West*, p. 62.

7. See I. P. Sheldon-Williams's helpful note on the use of this analogy in his edition of book I of the *Periphyseon, Iohannis Scotti Eriugenae Periphyseon*

Liber Primus, Scriptores Latini Hiberniae, vol. 7 (Dublin: Dublin Institute for Advanced Studies, 1968), p. 54.

8. The dialectical formulations used to great effect by Eriugena are typical of a negative approach to divine reality and derive ultimately from the Plotinian conception of the One; on Eriugena's concept of God and his affinity with and divergence from the Neoplatonists, see W. Beierwaltes, "Eriugena's Platonism," *Hermathena* 149 (1990), especially pp. 63–70.

9. See P. III 666D–667A; all translations of biblical texts are taken from the Revised Standard Version; these first four texts are again invoked in *Periphyseon* V (907B–908B).

10. In relation to the text of Genesis 1–3, Eriugena notes that the Trinity is openly revealed there (P. IV 786A–B); the importance of the hexaemeral commentary in the *Periphyseon* has prompted G.-H. Allard to state, perhaps a little extravagantly, that the whole of the *Periphyseon* can be understood as explanation of the text of Genesis; see "La structure littéraire de la composition du *De divisione naturae*," in *The Mind of Eriugena*, ed. J. J. O'Meara and L. Bieler (Dublin: Irish University Press, 1973), p. 147.

11. This translation of Ps. 110:3 is from the Vulgate since Eriugena's exegesis is based on the Latin version.

12. "'Magnorum Vivorum Quendam Consensum Velimus Machinari' (804D). Eriugena's use of Augustine's *De Genesi ad litteram* in the *Periphyseon*," in *Eriugena: Studien zu seinen Quellen*, ed. W. Beierwaltes (Heidelberg: Carl Winter Universitätsverlag, 1980), p. 115.

13. For a general discussion of this difficult theme in Eriugena's works, see W. Beierwaltes, "Unity and Trinity in East and West," in McGinn and Otten, *Eriugena East and West*, pp. 209–31, and "Unity and Trinity in Dionysius and Eriugena," *Hermathena* 157 (1994), pp. 1–20.

14. On this point, see Beierwaltes, "Unity and Trinity in East and West," pp. 219–23; see also P. W. Rosemann, *Omne Agens Agit Sibi Simile: A "Repetition" of Scholastic Metaphysics*, Louvain Philosophical Studies 12 (Leuven, Belgium: Leuven University Press, 1996), pp. 117–41, and J. Moreau, "Le Verbe et la création selon S. Augustin et J. S. Érigène," in *Jean Scot Érigène et l'histoire de la philosophie*, ed. R. Roques (Paris: CNRS, 1977), pp. 201–10.

15. See Augustine's *Literal Commentary on Genesis* I 9, 17 and *Answers to Eighty-Three Different Questions* 46. 1–2; according to R. D. Crouse, "the whole theological matrix of Eriugena's theory [of creation] was constituted by St. Augustine's exegesis of Genesis"; see "*Primordiales Causae* in Eriugena's Interpretation of Genesis: Sources and Significance," in *Iohannes Scottus Eriugena: The Bible and Hermeneutics*, ed. G. Van Riel, C. Steel, and J. J. McEvoy (Leuven, Belgium: Leuven University Press, 1996), p. 212.

16. The Dionysian treatise on the *Divine Names* is a detailed exposition of the names and principles of all things in God.

17. The Dionysian explanation of the unity and distinctions in the divine nature as the radii of a circle that meet in the center is in *Divine Names*, V 6.

18. P. II 550C and III 629A–693C; here Eriugena uses the term "darkness" in the Dionysian sense to indicate excellence, a use that is not always consistent in his works; I examine this issue in chapter 7.

19. "Divine Nothingness and Self-Creation in John Scottus Eriugena," p. 118; see also W. Beierwaltes, *"Negati Affirmatio:* Welt als Metapher," in Roques, *Jean Scot Érigène et l'histore de la philosophie,* pp. 263–75.

20. Sells, *Mystical Languages of Unsaying,* p. 60.

21. See *Celestial Hierarchy* 1.1; according to Sheldon-Williams, it is not clear if Dionysius had understood a distinction to exist between gift and grace; see his edition of book III of the *Periphyseon, Iohannis Scotti Eriugenae Periphyseon Liber Tertius,* Scriptores Latini Hiberniae, vol. 11 (Dublin: Dublin Institute for Advanced Studies, 1981), p. 309 n. 6; see also *Expositions on the Celestial Hierarchy* I 23–47.

22. On the generally neglected principles of negative theology in the thought of Augustine, see J. Heiser, "Saint Augustine and Negative Theology," *New Scholasticism* 53 (1989), pp. 66–80, and D. Carabine, "Negative Theology in the Thought of Saint Augustine," *Recherches de Théologie ancienne et médiévale* 59 (1992), pp. 5–22.

23. P. I 485B and IV 766B; see *On the Free Choice of the Will* II 12.

24. On the unnameability of God, see P. II 589C, where Eriugena uses the scriptural texts Judg. 13:18 and Phil. 2:9 in support of his argument; the simplicity and resulting ineffability of the divine nature are constant themes in the *Enneads* of Plotinus; see D. Carabine, *The Unknown God: Negative Theology in the Platonic Tradition: Plato to Eriugena* (Louvain, Belgium: Peeters, 1995), pp. 135–37.

25. *The Unknown God,* p. 305; on the methodologies of affirmation and their relationship between *scientia* and *sapientia,* see G. d'Onofrio, "The Concordia of Augustine and Dionysius: Towards a Hermeneutic of the Disagreement of Patristic Sources in John the Scot's *Periphyseon,*" in McGinn and Otten, *Eriugena East and West,* especially pp. 127–28.

26. Duclow, "Divine Nothingness and Self-Creation in John Scottus Eriugena," p. 112; on speaking about God, see D. J. O'Meara, "The Problem of Speaking about God in John Scottus Eriugena," in *Carolingian Essays: Andrew Mellon Lectures in Early Christian Studies,* ed. U.-R. Blumenthal (Washington, D.C.: Catholic University of America Press, 1983), pp. 151–67.

27. See J. C. Marler, "Dialectical Use of Authority in the *Periphyseon,*" in McGinn and Otten, *Eriugena East and West,* p. 102; see also B. McGinn's pertinent comments on this theme in "The Originality of Eriugena's Spiritual Exegesis," in Van Riel, Steel, and McEvoy, *Iohannes Scottus Eriugena: The Bible and Hermeneutics,* pp. 61–4.

28. See *The Unknown God,* pp. 311–16.

29. See Augustine's *On the Trinity* V 3 (4) and VII 4 (7).

30. Beierwaltes, *"Negati Affirmatio,"* p. 134; see also, by the same author, "Language and Object: Reflections on Eriugena's Valuation of the Function and Capabilities of Language," in *Jean Scot écrivain,* ed. G.-H. Allard (Montréal: Bellarmin, 1986), pp. 209–28.

31. *Anthropology,* pp. 59–62.

32. *Mystical Languages of Unsaying,* p. 59.

33. See *Derrida and Negative Theology,* ed. H. Coward and T. Foshay (Albany: SUNY Press, 1992), p. 76.

34. Sells, *Mystical Languages of Unsaying*, p. 44.

35. The One must be ignorant of itself in order to avoid duality; see *Enn.* III 8, 9, 15 and VI 9, 6, 12.

36. A. H. Armstrong makes this point in "Apophatic-Kataphatic Tensions in Religious Thought from the Third to the Sixth Century A.D.," in *From Augustine to Eriugena: Essays on Neoplatonism and Christianity in Honor of John O'Meara*, ed. F. X. Martin and J. A. Richmond (Washington, D.C.: Catholic University of America Press), p. 12.

Chapter 5

1. According to B. McGinn, Eriugena reinterprets Genesis from the perspective of *theologia* rather than *physica;* see "The Originality of Eriugena's Spiritual Exegesis," in *Iohannes Scottus Eriugena: The Bible and Hermeneutics*, ed. G. Van Riel, C. Steel, and J. J. McEvoy (Leuven, Belgium: Leuven University Press, 1996), especially pp. 68–72.

2. See J. Meyendorff, "Remarks on Eastern Patristic Thought in John Scottus Eriugena," in *Eriugena East and West*, ed. B. McGinn and W. Otten (Notre Dame, Indiana: University of Notre Dame Press, 1994), p. 59.

3. T. O'Loughlin, "Unexplored Irish Influence on Eriugena," *Recherches de Théologie ancienne et médiévale* 59(1992), p. 25.

4. See D. Moran's article on this subject, "'Officina omnium' or 'Notio quaedam intellectualis in mente divina aeternaliter facta'. The Problem of the Definition of Man in the Philosophy of John Scottus Eriugena," in *L'homme et son univers au moyen âge*, ed. C. Wenin (Louvain-la-Neuve: Éditions de l'Institut Supérieur de Philosophie, 1986), vol. 1, pp. 195–204.

5. Eriugena uses Mark 16:15 in support of his argument; see P. IV 755B and 760A; see also Jeauneau's note in his edition of book IV of the *Periphyseon, Iohannis Scotti: Eriugenae Periphyseon Liber Quartus*, Scriptores Latini Hiberniae, vol. 13 (Dublin: Dublin Institute for Advanced Studies, 1995), pp. 297–8 n. 91.

6. See W. Otten's comments on this theme in *The Anthropology of Johannes Scottus Eriugena*, Brill's Studies in Intellectual History 20 (Leiden: Brill, 1991), pp. 132–35.

7. On the various definitions of human nature, see Moran, "'Officina omnium,'" pp. 195–204.

8. See Otten's pertinent comments on this theme in *Anthropology*, p. 178.

9. "*Intelligo me esse:* Eriugena's '*Cogito*,'" in *Jean Scot Érigène et l'histoire de la philosophie*, ed. R. Roques (Paris: CNRS, 1977), p. 327.

10. *Anthropology*, pp. 185, 207–8, and 210–11; "*Intelligo me esse:* Eriugena's '*Cogito*,'" p. 334.

11. See D. Duclow's comments on this theme, especially in relation to Eriugena's *Commentary on the Celestial Hierarchy*, in "Isaiah Meets the Seraph: Breaking Ranks in Dionysius and Eriugena," in McGinn and Otten, *Eriugena East and West*, especially pp. 241–244.

12. On the different roles of the soul and the totality of things in human nature, see J. Pépin, "Humans and Animals: Aspects of Scriptural Reference in Eriugena's Anthropology," in McGinn and Otten, *Eriugena East and West*, p. 180.

Chapter 6

1. The theme of birth resulting in ignorance of the Good is also prominent in Plotinus (*Enn.* V 1, 1 and IV 8, 3–4) and Gregory of Nyssa (*On Virginity* X).

2. See W. Otten's comments on this theme in *The Anthropology of Johannes Scottus Eriugena*, Brill's Studies in Intellectual History 20 (Leiden: Brill, 1991), pp. 121–25, 146–49, and 193–94.

3. Ibid., pp. 147–48; see also pp. 154–55 and 194–96.

4. On Eriugena's interpretation of this Genesis text, see É. Jeauneau, "Jean Scot et l'ironie," in *Jean Scot écrivain*, ed. G.-H. Allard (Montréal: Bellarmin, 1986), pp. 13–27.

5. For an illuminating commentary on Eriugena's conception of the division of the sexes, see É. Jeauneau, "La division des sexes chez Grégoire de Nysse et chez Jean Scot Érigène," in *Études érigéniennes*, (Paris: Études augustiniennes, 1987), pp. 341–64.

6. Translation from J. J. O'Meara, *Eriugena*, (Oxford: Oxford University Press, 1989), p. 168; on the problem of knowledge and ignorance in relation to human nature, see W. Beierwaltes, "Das Problem des absoluten Selbstbewusstseins bei Johannes Scotus Eriugena," in *Platonismus in der Philosophie des Mittelalters*, Wege der Forschung, vol. 197 (Darmstadt: Wissenschaftliche Buchgesellschaft, 1969), pp. 484–516; reprinted in W. Beierwaltes, *Eriugena: Grundzüge seines Denkens* (Frankfurt am Main: Klostermann, 1994), pp. 180–203.

7. *Anthropology*, pp. 204–05.

8. On the concept of *homo absconditus*, see J. Saward, "Towards an Apophatic Anthropology," *Irish Theological Quarterly* 41 (1974), p. 229.

9. I am grateful to Philipp Rosemann for alerting me to this point.

10. *Anthropology*, p. 162.

11. See D. Duclow, "Denial or Promise of the Tree of Life? Eriugena, Augustine and Genesis 3:22b," in *Iohannes Scottus Eriugena: The Bible and Hermeneutics*, ed. G. Van Riel, C. Steel, and J. J. McEvoy (Leuven, Belgium: Leuven University Press, 1996), especially pp. 233–34.

12. See P. Dronke, "Eriugena's Earthly Paradise," in *Begriff und Metapher: Sprachform des Denkens bei Eriugena*, ed. W. Beierwaltes (Heidelberg: Carl Winter Universitätsverlag, 1990), especially pp. 218–19.

13. B. Stock, "The Philosophical Anthropology of Johannes Scottus Eriugena," *Studi medievali*, series 3, 8 (1967), p. 43.

14. See C. Steel, "The Tree of Knowledge of Good and Evil," in Van Riel, Steel, and McEvoy, *Iohannes Scottus Eriugena: The Bible and Hermeneutics*, pp. 246–55.

15. On this theme, see Otten, *Anthropology*, pp. 152–53.

16. According to W. Otten's analysis, the disappearance of a clear dividing line between what human nature was and what it is now because of sin means that it is impossible to distinguish between procession and reversion in relation to human nature; see Ibid., pp. 164–65.

17. Ibid., p. 179.

18. On the role of the Word and the perfection of human nature, see Stock, "The Philosophical Anthropology of Johannes Scottus Eriugena," especially pp. 9–12.

19. Ibid., p. 10.

20. On Eriugena's Christology, see E. Perl, "Metaphysics and Christology in Maximus the Confessor and Eriugena," in McGinn and Otten, *Eriugena East and West*, pp. 253–70.

21. See Jeauneau's note in his edition of book IV of the *Periphyseon, Iohannis Scotti Eriugenae Periphyseon Liber Quartus*, Scriptores Latini Hiberniae, vol. 13 (Dublin: Dublin Institute for Advanced Studies, 1995), p. 292 n. 70.

22. This is a prominent theme in Otten, *Anthropology*; see especially pp. 122–23 and p. 130.

23. É. Jeauneau, "Le thème du retour," in *Études érigéniennes*, p. 371.

24. W. Otten, "The Universe of Nature and the Universe of Man: Difference and Identity," in Beierwaltes, *Begriff und Metapher*, p. 206.

Chapter 7

1. See the final chapter of *Jean Scot Érigène, sa vie, son oeuvre, sa pensée* (Louvain, Belgium: Mont César, 1933).

2. P. V 900B–C and 952B; see S. Gersh's comments on this topic in "The Structure of the Return in Eriugena's *Periphyseon*," in *Begriff und Metapher: Sprachform das Denkens bei Eriugena* (Heidelberg: Carl Winter Universitätsverlag, 1990), especially pp. 110–11.

3. "Denial or Promise of the Tree of Life? Eriugena, Augustine and Genesis 3:22b," in *Iohannes Scottus Eriugena. The Bible and Hermeneutics*, ed. G. Van Riel, C. Steel, and J. J. McEvoy (Leuven, Belgium: Leuven University Press, 1996), especially pp. 228–34.

4. See P. I 526B–C; II 575A–C; III 684A; IV 747C–748C; V 895C, 912C–D, 902C–D.

5. "Metaphysics and Christology in Maximus the Confessor and Eriugena," in *Eriugena East and West*, ed. B. McGinn and W. Otten (Notre Dame, Indiana: Notre Dame University Press, 1994), especially p. 263 and pp. 265–67.

6. See C. Steel, "The Tree of Knowledge of Good and Evil," in Van Riel, Steel, and McEvoy, *Iohannes Scottus Eriugena: The Bible and Hermeneutics*, pp. 239–55.

7. See P. V 1011A–1018A; on this theme, see P. Dietricht and D. Duclow, "Virgins in Paradise. Deification and Exegesis in *Periphyseon* V," in *Jean Scot écrivain*, ed. G.-H. Allard (Montréal: Bellarmin, 1986), pp. 229–63, and D. Carabine, "Five Wise Virgins: *Theosis* and Return in *Periphyseon* V," in Van Riel, Steel, and McEvoy, *Iohannes Scottus Eriugena: The Bible and Hermeneutics*, especially pp. 200–204.

8. P. II 564B; III 656D, 664D, 684A; V 963C; see also *Aulae sidereae* 62–65 and *Hom.* XI 289D; XII 290A–B; on the metaphysics of light in Eriugena's thought, see J. J. McEvoy, "Metaphors of Light and Metaphysics of Light in Eriugena," in Beierwaltes, *Begriff und Metapher*, pp. 149–67.

9. D. Carabine, "Eriugena's Use of the Symbolism of Light, Cloud, and Darkness in the *Periphyseon*," in McGinn and Otten, *Eriugena East and West*, especially pp. 146–47.

10. On vision and theophany, see J. J. O'Meara, "Eriugena's Use of Augustine in his Teaching on the Return of the Soul and the Vision of God," in *Jean Scot Érigène et l'histoire de la philosophie*, ed. R. Roques (Paris: CNRS, 1977), pp. 191–200.

11. According to Gregory, since the divine nature is infinite, it follows that the search for God will be infinite; see *Against Eunomius* I 291 and *Life of Moses* II 239. This continual striving is what Jean Daniélou has described as *epectasis;* see *Platonisme et théologie mystique* (Paris: Aubier, Éditions Montaigne, 1944), pp. 309–33.

12. See P. III 668A–C, 614D–615A; the idea that God can be known as that but not what, is a strong theme in Gregory of Nyssa's Plotinian Platonism: see *Against Eunomius*, III vi, 8.

13. Translation from J. J. O'Meara, *Eriugena*, (Oxford: Oxford University Press, 1989), p. 161; on Eriugena's conception of the mystical ascent of Paul and John, see A. Kijewska,"The Eriugenian Concept of Theology: John the Evangelist as the Model Theologian," in Van Riel, Steel, and McEvoy, *Iohannes Scottus Eriugena: The Bible and Hermeneutics*, especially pp. 181–83.

14. P. V 876B, 913C, 926C–D, 945C–946A, 982C, 1020C–D; see also *Comm.* I xxv 302A–B; on the theme of "inaccessible light," see P. II 551C, 579B; III 633A, and 668C.

15. See T. Gregory, "L'eschatologie de Jean Scot," in Roques, *Jean Scot Érigène et l'histoire de la philosophie*, pp. 377–92.

In Retrospect

1. See W. Beierwaltes, ed., *Eriugena Redivivus: Zur Wirkungsgeschichte seines Denkens im Mittelalter und im Übergang zur Neuzeit* (Heidelberg: Care Winter Universitätsverlag, 1987), and the final chapters in D. Moran, *The Philosophy of John Scottus Eriugena* (Cambridge: Cambridge University Press, 1989), and J. J. O'Meara, *Eriugena*, (Oxford: Oxford University Press, 1989).

2. On the relevance of negative theology in contemporary times, see P. W. Rosemann, "Penser l'Autre: l'éthique de la théologie négative," *Revue Philosophique de Louvain* 93:3 (1995), pp. 408–27.

3. See *Dieu sans l'être* (Paris: Presses Universitaires de France; reprint, 1991); English translation: *God without Being*, trans. Thomas A. Carlson (Chicago: University of Chicago Press, 1991).

4. *The Glory of the Lord: A Theological Aesthetics*, vol. 4, *The Realm of Metaphysics in Antiquity* (Edinburgh: T. and T. Clark, 1989), pp. 343–44.

5. W. Beierwaltes, "Eriugena's Platonism," *Hermathena* 149 (1990), p. 53.

SUGGESTIONS FOR
FURTHER READING

A comprehensive, annotated bibliography can be found in M. Brennan, *A Guide to Eriugenian Studies: A Survey of Publications 1930–1987* (Fribourg, Switzerland: Éditions universitaires, 1989). A supplement to this bibliography covering the years 1987–96 has been compiled by G. Van Riel, "A Bibliographical Survey of Eriugenian Studies," in *Iohannes Scottus Eriugena: The Bible and Hermeneutics*, ed. G. Van Riel, C. Steel, and J. J. McEvoy (Leuven, Belgium: Leuven University Press, 1996), pp. 367–400. This bibliography is updated yearly in the *Annual Bulletin of the Society for the Promotion of Eriugenian Studies* (SPES), ed., J. J. McEvoy; see nos. 6 (1997), 7 (1998), and 8 (1999).

Serious publication on Eriugena (mostly in German and French) dates from the nineteenth century, and details of publications from 1823 to 1930 can be found in M. Cappuyns, *Jean Scot Érigène, sa vie, son oeuvre, sa pensée* (Louvain, Belgium: Mont César, 1933). Cappuyns's book is required reading for those who wish to investigate Eriugena further. The earliest monographs on Eriugena in English remained for more than half a century the only surveys in that language; see Alice Gardner, *Studies in John the Scot (Erigena): A Philosopher of the Dark Ages* (London: Oxford University Press, 1900), and Henry Bett, *Johannes Scotus Erigena: A Study in Medieval Philosophy* (Cambridge: Cambridge University Press, 1925). Although outdated in many respects, they do provide an insight into Eriugenian scholarship at the beginning of the twentieth century.

A very brief but eminently readable introduction to Eriugena can be found in J. J. O'Meara, *Eriugena*, Irish Life and Culture Series 17 (Cork: Mercier Press, 1969). This volume has long been out of print, but the author's more recent book gives a much more comprehensive account of the life and works of Eriugena and includes a translation of the *Homily on the Prologue of John*; see *Eriugena* (Oxford: Oxford University Press, 1989). Dermot Moran, *The Philosophy of John Scottus Eriugena: A Study of Idealism in the Middle Ages* (Cambridge: Cambridge University Press, 1989), is an interesting complement to O'Meara's work in that it approaches Eriugena from a contemporary perspective. Willemien Otten, *The Anthropology of Johannes Scottus Eriugena*, Brill's Studies in Intellectual History 20 (Leiden: Brill, 1991), does not restrict itself to an analysis of Eriugena's anthropology and provides a most illuminating account of many Eriugenian themes.

Although many articles published on Eriugena are scattered in various journals worldwide, the most accessible are the collections of conference papers from the various SPES colloquia. In these volumes, many leading Eriugenian scholars have greatly contributed to our current knowledge of Eriugena, in order of publication, as follows:

J. J. O'Meara and L. Bieler, eds. *The Mind of Eriugena*. Dublin: Irish University Press, 1973.

R. Roques, ed. *Jean Scot Érigène et l'histoire de la philosophie*. Paris: CNRS, 1977.

W. Beierwaltes, ed. *Eriugena: Studien zu seinen Quellen*. Heidelberg: Carl Winter Universitätsverlag, 1980.

G.-H. Allard, ed. *Jean Scot écrivain*. Montréal: Bellarmin, 1986.

W. Beierwaltes, ed. *Eriugena Redivivus: Zur Wirkungsgeschichte seines Denkens im Mittelalter und im Übergang zur Neuzeit*. Heidelberg: Care Winter Universitätsverlag, 1987.

C. Leonardi and E. Mesestò, eds. *Giovanni Scoto nel suo tempo: L'organizzazione del sapere in età carolingia*. Spoleto: Centro Italiano di Studi sull'Alto Medioeve, 1989.

W. Beierwaltes, ed. *Begriff und Metapher: Sprachform des Denkens bei Eriugena*. Heidelberg: Carl Winter Universitätsverlag, 1990.

B. McGinn and W. Otten, eds. *Eriugena East and West*. Notre Dame, Indiana: University of Notre Dame Press, 1994.

G. Van Riel, C. Steel, and J. J. McEvoy, eds. *Iohannes Scottus Eriugena: The Bible and Hermeneutics*. Leuven, Belgium: Leuven University Press, 1996.

Translations of Eriugena's works into English are still sadly lacking; those works that are available in single volumes are the *Periphyseon, On Predestination,* and the poetry; see I.P. Sheldon-Williams, revised by J. J. O'Meara, *Eriugena Periphyseon (The Division of Nature)*, Cahiers d'études médiévales, Cahier spécial 3 (Washington: Dumbarton Oaks, 1987); M. Brennan, trans., John Scottus Eriugena, *Treatise on Divine Predestination,* Notre Dame Texts in Medieval Culture 5 (Notre Dame, Indiana: University of Notre Dame Press, 1998), and M. Herren, *Iohannis Scoti Carmina*, Scriptores Latini Hiberniae, vol. 12 (Dublin: Dublin Institute for Advanced Studies, 1993).

INDEX